BRIDGE: TRIUMPHS AND DISASTERS

José Le Dentu has for many years been an outstanding figure in French bridge, with an equal reputation as player, author, journalist, magazine contributor, and bridgerama commentator. The present book contains some of his best writing in many fields. The five Parts relate to bidding, defence, dummy play, great catastrophes, and problems. A special feature is that all the deals are from actual play.

This version, a little shorter than the original, is by Terence Reese. It bears all the marks of his usual precision and wit.

D1579892

Also by Terence Reese

Do You Really Want to Win at Bridge?
(based on the French text by Pierre Béguin & Jean Besse)
Bridge for Ambitious Players

Mini-Masters
Master Plays in a Single Suit
Master Deceptive Plays

with Roger Trézel
Blocking and Unblocking Plays in Bridge
Safety Plays in Bridge
Elimination Plays in Bridge
Snares and Swindles in Bridge
Those Extra Chances in Bridge
When to Duck, When to Win in Bridge
Master the Odds in Bridge
The Art of Defence in Bridge
The Mistakes You Make at Bridge

with Rixi Markus
Better Bridge for Club Players

with David Bird
Miracles of Card Play
Unholy Tricks: More Miraculous Card Play
Doubled and Venerable: Further Miracles of Card Play
Bridge—Tricks of the Trade

with Julian Pottage
Positive Defence
Positive Declarer's Play

Bridge:
Triumphs and Disasters

José Le Dentu

English version by
Terence Reese

LONDON
VICTOR GOLLANCZ LTD
in association with
PETER CRAWLEY
1990

First published in Great Britain 1990
in association with Peter Crawley
by Victor Gollancz Ltd
14 Henrietta Street, London WC2E 8QJ

The source of this book is DONNES EXTRAORDINAIRES
by José Le Dentu published 1989 by
Editions Le Bridgeur, Paris, France

British Library Cataloguing in Publication Data
Le Dentu, José
    Bridge: triumphs and disasters.
    1. Contract bridge
    I. Title
    795.415

    ISBN 0–575–04806–9

Photoset in Great Britain by
Rowland Phototypesetting Ltd, Bury St Edmunds, Suffolk
and printed by St Edmundsbury Press Ltd
Bury St Edmunds, Suffolk

Contents

Foreword
by José Le Dentu

The aim of this book is clear: to give pleasure to bridge players while commenting on the most interesting aspects of the game.

The logical order has been to begin with bidding situations (Part I), to follow with leads and defence (Part II), then declarer's play (Part III), great catastrophes (Part IV), and finally some problem deals (Part V).

The first task has been to make a selection from thousands of hands, the second to classify them. For the most part I have described them in chronological order to preserve their historical context.

Each of the examples is headed by an appropriate title, and in most chapters I have concluded with a 'point to remember'.

The various deals are independent of one another, so you may read wherever the fancy takes you. If you find the hands entertaining, this will be an excellent way to improve your game.

José Le Dentu

Terence Reese adds:
Like a number of British players, Le Dentu passed his university and legal examinations with distinction, then revived a childhood interest in bridge. In a career not dissimilar from my own, he became an international player, then a full-time author, journalist, magazine contributor, and bridgerama commentator.

The present book reflects his experience in many fields. The text is shorter than in the original French version, but I have selected the best plums from the basket.

One feature you will appreciate is that you will never need to turn back to the preceding page to remind yourself what the deal is about.

Part I is derived from José's long stint as competition editor of various French magazines. Most of the problems deal with apparently simple, but nevertheless instructive, situations. From time to time I have expanded, and on some occasions disputed, his analysis. But then, you wouldn't expect two bridge experts to agree with one another all the time, would you?

My colleague in various books, David Bird, has read the text of this one and has made many perceptive comments.

PART I

We Hear from the Experts

In this first part, famous players from France and other countries answer problems that I have set over the years in the competition pages of the *Revue Française de Bridge*, and its successor, *Le Bridgeur*.

Some of the answers will surprise you. But there is nothing surprising in that, because the problems are of the sort that lead to many differences of opinion.

If certain experts are on occasions rather too categorical in their answers, it is because what the lawyers call 'reasonable doubt' is not their principal quality.*

So as not to lose the common touch, I have also taken note of the opinions of a small group of non-expert players.

If at times I have been slightly ironic, not to say caustic, in my comments, it is because a smack in the eye for the experts gives a lot of pleasure to average players.

There are fifteen problems in this section, with a score of 100 for the best (usually the most popular) answer. If it would amuse you to see how you would have fared if you had been on the panel, this is my rough assessment:

> 1250 points (out of 1500): very strong.
> 1000 points: useful.
> 750 points: keep trying.

* Oh dear, is he getting at me?—T.R.

Responding on a Minimum

At love all the bidding goes:

South	West	North	East
—	—	1◇	No
?			

What should South call, holding:

♠ A 8 7 6 2   ♡ 9 8 2   ◇ 10 3   ♣ 8 5 2

What is the minimum on which you should respond to an opening bid of one? Three-quarters of the panel advised one spade.

MONK: 1♠. You are a point short (assuming that the normal minimum is 5), but if you don't speak now you may never have a chance. If the hand is eventually played in a suit contract your ace will be valuable, and at notrumps it will be a sure entry card.

DELMOULY chose 1♠, adding: The advantages and the disadvantages work out about equal.

ROUDINESCO was more decisive: 1♠. An ace, a five-card major, and the (so far) silent opposition are three good reasons to speak on a sub-minimum.

DELORME: 1♠. In our antediluvian system partner might hold 23 points (counting distribution).

No longer, surely. There was a time when players used to open with a bid of one on giants, but nowadays there are other ways of expressing such hands.

SAUMUR: 1♠. Confucius he say, conceal bad hand.

The general opinion was that it is right to respond one spade at pairs or teams, but wiser to pass at rubber bridge. As CALIX remarked: There is a risk that you may find you have embarked on a slave-ship, with no control over your destiny.

Marks: One spade, 100; pass, 80. (30 votes for 1♠, 9 for pass.)
Point to remember: It is reasonable to respond on a five-card suit headed by the ace, which will at least supply one trick and an entry card.

The hand in question was held by North on a deal from the Philip Morris at Zurich in 1979. There was an intervening bid and so no question of North giving a free response.

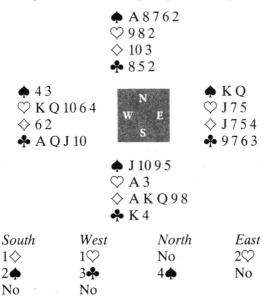

♠ A 8 7 6 2
♡ 9 8 2
◇ 10 3
♣ 8 5 2

♠ 4 3
♡ K Q 10 6 4
◇ 6 2
♣ A Q J 10

♠ K Q
♡ J 7 5
◇ J 7 5 4
♣ 9 7 6 3

♠ J 10 9 5
♡ A 3
◇ A K Q 9 8
♣ K 4

South	West	North	East
1◇	1♡	No	2♡
2♠	3♣	4♠	No
No	No		

There seem to be four top losers, but South played cleverly. He won the second heart and cashed ◇ A, unblocking dummy's 10. After a spade to the ace he finessed ◇ 9, since East was likely to hold the length in diamonds. The third diamond was ruffed by West and overruffed.

South regained entry by ruffing the third heart, and two clubs went away on the long diamonds. The defence was held to one spade, one heart and one club.

Responding with 4-4 in the Reds

At game all the bidding goes:

South	West	North	East
—	—	1♣	No
?			

What should South call, holding:

♠ K 7 6
♡ A Q 9 6
♢ K 6 4 2
♣ 7 3

North-South are playing five-card majors.

With four hearts and four diamonds is it right to respond
one heart or one diamond?

When the five-card major systems such as Roth-Stone and
Kaplan-Sheinwold were developed in the 1950s it was considered obligatory to respond one heart, since otherwise the
possible 4-4 fit in a major might be missed. Sheinwold even
quoted this assortment,

♠ 7 6
♡ 6 5 4 3
♢ A K 8 7 4
♣ K 4

with the recommendation to respond one heart.

The system has changed since negative (originally sputnik)
doubles were invented. Take a sequence such as:

South	West	North	East
—	—	1♣	No
1♢	1♠	No	2♠
?			

At this point a double by South would not be for penalties and would imply (though not guarantee) four hearts.

The usual style nowadays with 4-4 in the red suits is to respond one heart on moderate hands worth only one bid, and one diamond with upwards of 10 points. Thus:

MOLLO and DELMOULY: 1♦. Always one heart with poor or average hands, one diamond with good hands.

TRÉZEL and REESE: 1♦. On the next round jump in notrumps, with a good chance of attracting a heart lead.

CHEMLA: 1♦, the 'book' bid. But quite often at the table I would choose one heart.

Oh well, he likes to play the hand.

CARCY: 1♡. I like to name the major suit in case the opponents contest in spades.

GALULA: 1♡. The idea of up-the-line bidding has no sound base to it, despite the insistence of its supporters.

CALABRO: 1♡. Why do you ask this question?

As you see, there are different opinions. Habits have changed since the early years. Recently a Bridge World panel voted by a big majority for one heart over one club on:

♠ 8 5 3
♡ K J 6 2
♦ K J 6 2
♣ 10 2

But in answer to a supplementary question they added that with ace of clubs instead of the 10 they would respond one diamond.

Marks: One diamond, 100; one heart, 80; 2NT, 40; 3NT, 30. (27 votes for 1♦, 15 for 1♡, 1 for 2NT.)

Point to remember: When your partner has opened one club and you hold two four-card suits (not spades and hearts), normally respond in the higher suit on moderate hands worth only one bid and in the lower suit with 10 points or more. With spades and hearts, almost always respond one heart.

Choosing the Suit for a Trial Bid

At game all the bidding goes:

South	West	North	East
1♠	No	2♠	No
?			

What should South call, holding:

> ♠ A K 7 6 2
> ♡ A 5 2
> ♢ 6 4
> ♣ A 7 3

Yet again one finds that one expert in three is completely intoxicated by the number of points in the hand.

Carrying the flag for the passers, GRESH writes: Pass, with 15 points and too many losers.

The way to look at it is this: (i) After a single raise should you bid again with upwards of 17 points? Yes, they cry. (ii) What is the South hand worth when you have been raised in spades? Answer, close to 18.

In the 4-3-2-1 count working aces are undervalued. You may add half a point for each one. Also, you hold a five-card suit and have found a fit, so surely 'around 18 points' is no exaggeration.

Some theorists might point to the number of losers. This sort of calculation is based on moving sands. With these controls, who can say where the losers will be? (J 10 9 opposite x x x is worth nothing, but J 10 9 opposite A x x is likely to be worth two tricks.) As I said, the hand is as good as many containing 18 points. To calculate in any other way is playing blind man's buff.

ANON: Pass. No chance for game unless partner has extra values.

Just give North a singleton in hearts or clubs, and already you will be close to ten tricks.

MOLLO: 3♣. My hand is worth 17 to 18 . . .

The majority chose to rebid. There were 12 votes for three clubs, including:

DELMOULY: 3♣. The excellent controls justify a game try, the more so as you are vulnerable. Four trumps in North and something like K Q x x x in hearts or clubs might alone produce 11 tricks, and there are innumerable other possibilities.

Other members of the panel prefer 2NT, describing this as a general game try.

A slight disadvantage of 2NT, it seems to me, is that if partner, with scattered values, were to raise to 3NT, this contract would be played by the wrong hand, especially if North held such as Q x in hearts or clubs or K x x in diamonds. (Of course, you can go back to four spades.)

North's hand at the table was:

♠ Q 8 4 3
♡ K Q 7 6
♢ 8 7 5
♣ 8 4

Over three clubs he would probably try three hearts, which would encourage the opener to go to game. Meanwhile, 12 of our panel remain buried in two spades!

Marks: 2NT or three clubs, 100; pass, 50; three spades, 40; four spades, 30. (12 votes for 3♣, 12 for pass, 12 for 2NT, 2 for 3♠.)

Point to remember: Always assign extra values, after suit agreement, to aces and kings. Generally, make a game try with 17 or with 16 and good distribution.

Terrorist Action

Pairs, E–W vulnerable, the bidding goes:

South	West	North	East
—	—	1◇	No
?			

What should South call, holding:

♠ J 10 9 7 5 4 3
♡ 4 3
◇ 4 3
♣ 8 2

TRÉZEL: 1♠. What's the problem?

GALULA: Pass, and I am tempted to say that any other response would be an insult to partner.

DELMOULY: 3♠, a normal risk at pairs. I might pass in some circumstances, but I would never respond one spade, which might lead to sequences quite out of control.

So there are three possible choices!

CHEMLA: 3♠, a terrorist action perhaps, but at pairs I expect my partner to proceed with caution.

BESSE: 3♠. Likely to be more effective than pass or one spade; dangerous only if North has a big hand with a singleton spade.

MOLLO: 3♠, to annoy West.

DELORME: 3♠. After that, I shall not speak again.

Not meaning quite that, I dare say. More than two-thirds of the jury decided to respond, but those who voted for one spade were not entirely happy.

BESSE: 1♠. It's surely right to say something, but let's keep our heads.

ROUDINESCO: 1♠. One wants at least Q J or king of spades to bid three.

Twelve members of the jury voted for Pass, and REESE

explains why: It is best to pass and listen. The suit is too poor for three spades, and one spade can lead to all kinds of problem.

CAMPBELL: Pass. After all, the fourth player is likely to reopen.

So what is the least evil? Probably three spades. A correspondent described an occasion when at many tables South passed and a reasonable game was missed because the opener held:

♠ Q 6
♡ A Q 7
♢ A K 10 8 6 2
♣ A 5

At some tables, apparently, North opened two diamonds and the game was still missed. Nowadays, of course, an opening two diamonds (unless a weak two) would be forcing for one round at least.

Marks: Three spades, 100; one spade, 80; pass, 70; four spades, 20. (18 votes for 3♠, 13 for 1♠, 12 for pass.)

Point to remember: A double jump over an opening bid of one indicates a weak hand with a seven-card suit, preferably headed by two honours. It is a defensive bid and the opener will pass unless particularly strong.

T.R. adds: If (as José suggests) the response of three spades might be made on a seven-card suit headed by K Q, it seems to me unsound to make it on so weak a hand as this one. My own view of these situations is that it is foolish to pre-empt wildly when your partner has opened the bidding and there is no reason to assume that the opponents can make a game.

Minor-suit Fit after Stayman

Pairs, love all, the bidding goes:

South	West	North	East
—	—	1NT	No
2♣	No	2♦	No
?			

What should South call, holding:

♠ A 10 7 6
♡ 4
♦ Q J 10 2
♣ K J 10 6

You are playing a strong notrump, so there must be a good game contract somewhere. You know the opponents have at least nine hearts between them, so is it sensible to bid 3NT?

CHEMLA: 3♣ The fact that you are playing in a pairs does not justify an atrocity such as 3NT.

How, then, do you prepare the ground for a better contract on the occasions when partner does not hold a double stop in hearts?

It is possible, over two diamonds, to bid three diamonds, inviting partner to name a three-card major, but this style does not help you to find a good contract in a minor. You can do this by bidding three clubs over two diamonds. This is not a sign off in clubs: it asks the opener to develop his hand in a natural way, taking into account that he has already denied a four-card major. The opener follows this general scheme of rebids:

1. 3♦ with four diamonds, 3NT with four clubs.
2. 3♡ or 3♠ with a good three-card holding.
3. 4♣ or 4♦ with a five-card suit.

This is a sound and simple method, but when the present problem was put to an American panel the answers were:

[18]

19 for 3NT, 8 for 3$\diamondsuit$, 7 for 3♣, and others . . .

You can see the weakness of 3NT if you credit the opener with such as:

♠ K 8
♡ J 8 5
$\diamondsuit$ A K 6 3
♣ A Q 9 4

One down (at least) in 3NT instead of a slam in either minor!

DELMOULY: 3♣ forcing. There might be a slam in a minor and you might go down in 3NT.

Note, also, that if partner held such as A x x in hearts, 3NT might still produce a calamitous result.

Marks: Three clubs, 100; 3NT, 80; three diamonds, 50. (10 votes for 3♣, 9 for 3NT, 3 for 3$\diamondsuit$.)

Point to remember: In tournament play, especially, it is essential, after a Stayman two clubs has produced a negative reply, to use three clubs for inquiry, not as a sign-off.

When to Give Preference

Teams, love all, the bidding goes:

South	West	North	East
—	—	1♠	No
1NT	No	2◇	No
?			

What should South call, holding:

♠ Q 3
♡ 5 2
◇ Q J 10 5
♣ J 9 4 3 2

At first glance three responses seem possible—pass, two spades, three diamonds. On inspection, one seems better than the others. Let us take a look at the good and bad points:

Pass has two disadvantages. If partner is weak you are giving West a chance to come in with two hearts and perhaps have the better of the exchanges. Equally, if partner is close to maximum for his sequence, you may be missing a game.

Three diamonds. You are not worth it and may be transforming a plus score into a minus.

Two spades. An important advantage of this preference bid is that you prevent West from contesting with two hearts; also, there may be a game if partner can bid again.

Nevertheless, pass and three diamonds obtained a large majority from the panel.

GIRARDIN: Pass. But in a pairs I would say two spades.

PARIENTE: Pass, though game is not impossible.

TINTNER and FILARSKI: 3◇. But where are the hearts?

BESSE: 3◇. If partner is weak, make it more difficult for them to come in; if he is strong, game is possible.

There were only five votes for two spades, although partner, on this sequence, must hold five.

DELMOULY: 2♠. An old argument. You are not worth three diamonds and I don't like to pass for two reasons: four spades may be on and I don't want to give them a chance to compete in hearts.

Quite right, as you will see from the full deal, from the qualifying round of the world championship in Manila:

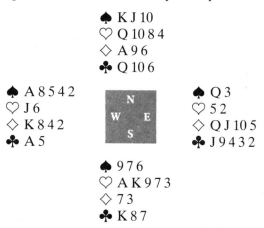

     ♠ K J 10
     ♡ Q 10 8 4
     ◇ A 9 6
     ♣ Q 10 6

♠ A 8 5 4 2   ♠ Q 3
♡ J 6   ♡ 5 2
◇ K 8 4 2   ◇ Q J 10 5
♣ A 5   ♣ J 9 4 3 2

     ♠ 9 7 6
     ♡ A K 9 7 3
     ◇ 7 3
     ♣ K 8 7

Two American teams were in opposition. After the sequence we have been discussing, East at one table passed two diamonds. South came in with two hearts and North raised to four hearts. West began with ace and another spade. South went up with the king in dummy and made the contract quite easily, playing West for A x in clubs.

At the other table Hamilton, East, bid two spades over his partner's two diamonds. This was made for a score of 110 and a swing of 11 match points.

Incidentally, after one spade—1NT, do you approve of West's two diamonds? It is usually better to pass 1NT on such holdings, especially when you are playing five-card majors.

Marks: Two spades, 100; pass or three diamonds, 80. (11 votes for pass, 7 for 3◇, 5 for 2♠.)

Point to remember: In the part-score region consider always the best strategy to obtain the contract.

[21]

Opening 1NT with a Six-card Minor

Teams, love all, the bidding goes:

South	West	North	East
—	—	—	No
1NT	3♠	4♠	No
?			

What should South call, holding:

♠ K J
♡ Q 9 7
♢ A K J 10 4 2
♣ Q 3

It is not so unusual to open a strong 1NT with a six-card minor. Having done so here, should South regret it?

BESSE: 5♢. South would prefer now to have opened one diamond, but 1NT was a perfectly good choice.

CALABRO looks on the bright side: 5♢. For once I have opened 1NT with a powerful six-card suit, and now I have the chance to name it!

No doubt, but how will partner know that you have a six-card suit as opposed to a four-card suit? Personally, I would have jumped to six diamonds, as proposed by seven of the panel.

DELMOULY: 6♢. North has forced me to bid at the five level. With this fine suit I can bid six despite the poor controls. North must have a fit for diamonds together with an ace and an ace-king in the two other suits.

There might possibly be two aces to lose, and for this reason a few panelists voted for 4NT. But unlucky! 4NT would be natural now.

POTIER: 5♢, which doesn't stop North going to six.

The deal occurred in the 1962 world championship, won by

the Italian Blue Team. The slam was lay-down. The Canadian Eric Murray bid 4NT with rather unfortunate consequences.

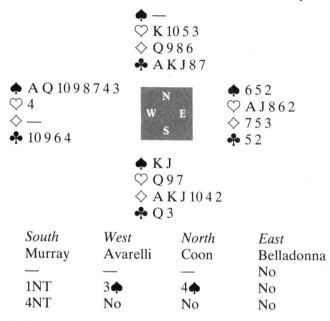

♠ —
♡ K 10 5 3
◇ Q 9 8 6
♣ A K J 8 7

♠ A Q 10 9 8 7 4 3
♡ 4
◇ —
♣ 10 9 6 4

♠ 6 5 2
♡ A J 8 6 2
◇ 7 5 3
♣ 5 2

♠ K J
♡ Q 9 7
◇ A K J 10 4 2
♣ Q 3

South	West	North	East
Murray	Avarelli	Coon	Belladonna
—	—	—	No
1NT	3♠	4♠	No
4NT	No	No	No

Walter found the heart lead—for six down! At the other table Kay and Nail defended in six spades over six diamonds and were two down.

Note that East's ace of hearts, at the first table, was worth nine tricks all on its own!

Marks: Six diamonds, 100; five diamonds, 90; 4NT, 30. (14 votes for 5◇, 7 for 6◇, 4 for 4NT.)

Point to remember: With a six-card minor, about 16 points, and honours in all the other suits, it is perfectly in order to open a strong 1NT.

Versatile Performance

Teams, N–S vulnerable, the bidding goes:

South	West	North	East
1♣	No	1♡	No
?			

What should South call, holding:

♠ Q 8
♡ A Q 4
♢ J 4
♣ A K 10 9 7 3

This is an awkward hand. You might open 1NT (as in the preceding example), but this seems doubtful with two weak doubletons. After the one club opening and the one heart response, the rebid is debatable.

CHEMLA: 2♣. Some survivors from prehistoric times will no doubt suggest three clubs or two hearts.

DELMOULY: 3♣. I refuse to bid just two clubs, even if some people regard this as modern science.

BESSE: 2♢, because three clubs may make it awkward for North to repeat his hearts or bid 3NT.

FILARSKI: 3♡. The most natural bid, the best bid . . . and the one most open to argument.

REESE: 3♣. The only danger is that partner may pass three clubs with a fair suit of hearts. (S. J. Simon used to recommend two hearts on this type of hand, but you are a bit good for that.)

TINTNER and MEYER: 2♣. The modern tendency is to treat this rebid of a minor as variable.

You may wonder what happened at the table. I held the North hand, playing with Rixi Markus in a rubber bridge game during the Marbella festival.

```
                    ♠ A 7 3
                    ♡ K 10 8 6 5
                    ◇ A K 3 2
                    ♣ J
   ♠ K 10 4              N              ♠ J 9 6 5 2
   ♡ 7 3          W          E         ♡ J 9 2
   ◇ Q 9 6              S              ◇ 10 8 7 5
   ♣ Q 8 5 4 2                         ♣ 6
                    ♠ Q 8
                    ♡ A Q 4
                    ◇ J 4
                    ♣ A K 10 9 7 3
```

South	West	North	East
Rixi	X . . .	Le Dentu	Y . . .
1♣	No	1♡	No
1♠ (!)	No	3◇	No
4♡	No	4♠	No
5♣	No	6♡	all pass

East led his singleton club. I won with the ace and ran the 10 of clubs, which East ruffed (though it might have been better play not to). I won the spade return, crossed to ♡ Q, ruffed a club with ♡ K, and drew the remaining trumps. Now another club ruff, diamond ruff, and I had enough tricks.

I later posed the problem in *Le Bridgeur*. Rixi's answer: 3♡, but if my partner is French I will say three clubs because they always respond one heart with four small.

Evidently Rixi took me for one of the Spaniards in Marbella —or perhaps as a visitor from Outer Space!

Marks: Three clubs or two clubs, 100; three hearts, 80; two diamonds, 70; one spade or two hearts, 60. (14 votes for 3♣, 7 for 2♣, 2 for 3♡ or 2◇.)

Point to remember: The sequence 1♣-any-2♣ should have a wide range. The reason is that 1♣-any-3♣ has to include a number of rather strong hands on which the player would have preferred to open with a two-bid.

Optimistic Assessment

At love all the bidding goes:

South	West	North	East
—	No	2NT	No
3♡	No	4♣	No
?			

South's 3♡ is a transfer bid and North's 4♣ is a slam try, confirming spades.

What should South call, holding:

♠ K 10 9 7 6 5   ♡ 10   ◇ J 10 4 3   ♣ Q 6

Do bridge players tend to set their sights on distant skies?

South has made a transfer bid here because it would be better for North to be the declarer, but has he any reason to expect a slam? For six spades to be a good contract, North would need to have an excellent fit, something like:

$$A J x \qquad A x x \qquad K Q x \qquad A K x x$$

Even now you will need to pick up the queen of spades and escape a possible ruff in diamonds. So the slam is scarcely better than a 50-50 chance. And, of course, it is not profitable to construct hands for partner when there are many thousands of possible holdings.

How many panelists out of 34 do you think were content to bid just four spades over four clubs? Only four!

There were 25 votes for four hearts, which, it is true, does not of itself carry you too high. And since North, at the table, held A K x of hearts, he might realise that there was duplication. Some panelists were not even content with four hearts as a slam suggestion. Thus:

CARCY: 4NT, to avoid any misunderstanding. Unless we are missing two aces I will bid the slam.

And 4NT was the player's selection when the hand occurred in the 1982 American team championship.

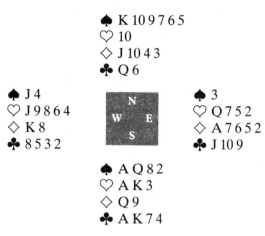

```
                    ♠ K 10 9 7 6 5
                    ♡ 10
                    ♢ J 10 4 3
                    ♣ Q 6
   ♠ J 4                              ♠ 3
   ♡ J 9 8 6 4         N              ♡ Q 7 5 2
   ♢ K 8            W     E           ♢ A 7 6 5 2
   ♣ 8 5 3 2           S             ♣ J 10 9
                    ♠ A Q 8 2
                    ♡ A K 3
                    ♢ Q 9
                    ♣ A K 7 4
```

South	West	North	East
Crane	Dupont	Sanders	Garozzo
—	—	—	No
2NT	No	3♡	No
4♣	No	4NT	No
5♠	No	6♠	all pass

West led a heart to the queen and ace. South drew trumps in two rounds, finishing on the table. What next, do you think?

Barry Crane led a low diamond from dummy. East went in with the ace and led a club. South won in dummy, came to hand with a trump to cash the king of hearts, then played off all the trumps. West, with the king of diamonds and the long clubs, was squeezed.

East's play of the ace of diamonds looks wrong and having done this he might have played a second round. But don't be too critical. After all, East was . . . Garozzo.

Marks: Four hearts or four spades, 100; four diamonds or 4NT, 60; five spades, 40. (25 votes for 4♡, 4 for 4♠, 2 for 4NT, 1 each for 4♡ and 5♠.)

Point to remember: If you are thinking of a slam try, avoid it if there is any danger that you may go down in five.

Burst of Enthusiasm

Teams, N–S vulnerable, the bidding goes:

South	West	North	East
1♣	No	1♢	1♡
?			

What should South call, holding:

> ♠ 8 6 3
> ♡ A Q 7
> ♢ 9
> ♣ A K Q 10 7 4

First of all, it is well to appreciate that the South hand is worth more than the 15 points in high cards: you must take note of the well-placed honours in hearts and the nearly solid club suit.

The next question is to determine the relative meanings of 2NT and 3NT in this kind of sequence. One view is expressed by:

BESSE, PILON, and DELMOULY: 3NT. This bid, after an opening one club, is more of a tactical bid than a value call. It suggests less in high cards than 2NT. You probably have eight playing tricks in your own hand.

VELUT: 3NT, though it is true that 2NT leaves open more possibilities.

But both 2NT and 3NT suggest rather better all-round values. A further point is that the club suit will not necessarily run. Thus:

ROUDINESCO: 3♣. I don't like 3NT. You would need the jack of clubs (instead of the 10) to stand a double.

Not to mention a guard in spades!

TINTNER: 3♣. In match play you have to be fairly serious and not try to steal game in notrumps.

DELORME: 3♣. This seems to me more judicious than pass or two clubs.

Pass? Is that some sort of inter-planetary psychic? There was some support, also, for one spade, no doubt to prevent a lead in that suit, but meanwhile partner will hardly place you with three small spades and six good clubs. Now see what happened at the table:

'I was South', writes NOLOT, 'and I bid 2NT. This produced four diamonds from my partner, who held:

♠ K Q 7 4   ♡ —   ◇ K Q J 10 7 4 2   ♣ 6 5

'After that it wasn't possible to stop the machine. I bid four hearts, he 4NT; then came five hearts (two aces), five spades, 5NT, where at last we stopped. This was one down.'

It would have been wiser to pass 4NT or perhaps bid five clubs. When you have overbid you sometimes have to 'lie' over 4NT.

Marks: Three clubs, 100; 3NT, 80; 2NT, 70; one spade, 40; 1NT or two clubs or two hearts, 30. (18 votes for 3♣, 10 for 3NT, 4 from 2NT, 2 for 1♠ or 2♣ or 2♡, 1 for 1NT.)

Point to remember: When you have overbid somewhat, you have to stop the engine as soon as you can. It is perfectly in order to lie over Blackwood so long as you don't appear to hesitate (which would tell partner what you were doing). Also, you are at no point obliged to inform the opposition.

Responding to an Overcall

Pairs, love all, the bidding goes:

South	West	North	East
—	1♣	1♦	No
?			

What should South call, holding:

> ♠ A K 7 6
> ♡ K 8 6 4
> ♦ 8 5 3
> ♣ 6 4

It may seem a simple affair at a low level, but the panel split in four directions.

SAUMUR: 1♡. What's the problem? I make the same reply as to an opening bid, telling my partner meanwhile that I have fair values.

POTIER: 2♦. One heart opens up more possibilities, but two diamonds is the safe way to start.

The disadvantage of one heart (as we shall see later) is that it may be inconvenient if partner raises.

CHEMLA: 1♡. Natural and forcing. At the level of one the bidding after an overcall is much the same as after an opening bid.

Is that right? Suppose you held something like J x x x in hearts: would you then bid one heart in response to an overcall? I can imagine Paul saying: 'Did you confuse the spades and the hearts? Or did you think I *opened* one diamond?' FRENDO and MONK were two who preferred to respond one spade because the hearts were so weak.

By no means everyone would agree that one heart (or one spade) was forcing. Fortunately there is a sound alternative:

ROUDINESCO and BESSE: 2♣. This is like a negative double when an opponent has intervened. The cue-bid is no *grande chose*, but it shows values.

CALULA: 2♣, asking partner to name a major if he has one.

REESE: 2♣, to indicate that your side holds the majority of the points.

The hand is minimum for the cue-bid, it is true, but safe enough if you play it as forcing for one round only. One advantage of this method is that if you hold a strong suit of clubs you can overcall with two clubs and follow with three clubs, trusting partner to understand. Perhaps because of possible misunderstandings in this area, there was good support for two diamonds:

FINK and FILARSKI: 2♢, not strong enough for two clubs.

The hand occurred during selection trials for the mixed pairs in the 1982 Olympiad. PALADINO bid one heart over partner's one diamond. Unfortunately the next player jumped to three clubs and North, quite reasonably, bid three hearts on:

♠ Q 10 8 4
♡ Q 7 3
♢ A K Q 7 4
♣ 5

So they missed a game in spades, because South hurriedly passed three hearts. As you see, the cue-bid of two clubs would have worked better.

Marks: Two clubs, 100; one heart or two diamonds, 80; one spade, 60. (13 votes for 2♣, 9 for 1♡, 8 for 2♢, 2 for 1♠.)

Point to remember: The cue-bid in this sequence is not a big bid: it is just a way of finding the best contract.

A Change of Style

Pairs, love all, the bidding goes:

South	West	North	East
—	No	No	1♣
?			

What should South call, holding:

♠ A Q
♡ K Q 10 3
♢ K 10 9 2
♣ 8 5 3

There are three possibilities—pass, double, one heart.

Back in 1964 I wrote in one of the magazines: Must the second player refrain from doubling when he holds only two cards in the highest-valued suit? On the present hand is it better to pass or bid one heart rather than double?

The experts then were happy to double. For example:

BESSE: Double. You can't always have four spades and a singleton club.

DESROUSSEAUX: Double. It's against my principles; but at least the spades are good ones.

On the other side of the fence, ROMANET considered that an overcall of one heart was the lesser evil, while SUSSEL declared 'No problem—pass'. However, that style of strong pass went out of fashion many years ago. When I set the problem again twenty years later there was a big majority for one heart.

CHEMLA: 1♡. You must not, not, not double with this type of hand. Even the Italians have abandoned that idea.

Not altogether, for:

AVARELLI and PABIS-TICCI: Double. Avarelli adds: If North jumps to four spades, A Q will be adequate support. At one time Italian players completely ignored the concept of preparedness: the system was simply to double when the hand contained the values for an opening bid. They have now moved some way from that, admitting that preparedness in the top suit is desirable.

ROUDINESCO: 1♡. You may not like this overcall in a four-card suit, but good players have been doing it for many years.

Marks: One heart, 100; double, 70; pass, 50. (24 votes for 1♡, 8 for pass, 7 for double.)

Point to note: Unless the hand is particularly strong, do not double with only two cards in the top suit; at the one-level prefer to overcall in a four-card suit.

Bird in the Hand

Rubber bridge, N–S vulnerable, the bidding goes:

South	West	North	East
—	—	—	2♠*
Dble	3♡	No	No
?		*weak, 7–11	

What should South call, holding:

♠ A   ♡ A K Q 10 3   ♢ 9 5 2   ♣ A K 4 3

A veteran of the rubber bridge game as well as of duplicate,
JEAN BESSE writes: Better a bird in the hand than two in the
bush. I pass. Don't forget the 100 honours!

POTIER: Double. Sometimes they all pass.

CALABRO: 3♠, a cue-bid, to be followed by four hearts.

REESE: 3NT. You can hardly expect to defend against three
hearts doubled!

ECKER: Pass. It wouldn't occur to me to snatch the bread
from my own mouth.

But the majority chose to double.

DELMOULY: Double. Too bad if I have lost the only chance
to record a plus score. The double is not ambiguous,
because if I wanted my partner to speak I would bid three
spades.

TINTNER does his sums: Double. West, obviously, is being
funny and has some support for spades. Six down un-
doubled, not vulnerable, even with 100 honours, might
bring in less than a penalty double of four spades (assuming
they eventually sacrifice).

The hand was played in Shanghai on the occasion of an
American visit in 1981. Alan Truscott wrote in the *New York
Sunday Times*: Several famous men have enjoyed a game of
bridge . . . Churchill . . . Eisenhower . . . and vice-president

Deng Xiaoping, who finds the game a perfect distraction, as the following hand shows:

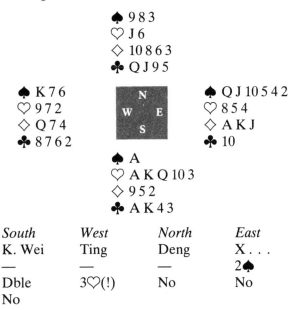

```
                    ♠ 9 8 3
                    ♡ J 6
                    ♢ 10 8 6 3
                    ♣ Q J 9 5
  ♠ K 7 6                          ♠ Q J 10 5 4 2
  ♡ 9 7 2          N               ♡ 8 5 4
  ♢ Q 7 4        W   E             ♢ A K J
  ♣ 8 7 6 2          S             ♣ 10
                    ♠ A
                    ♡ A K Q 10 3
                    ♢ 9 5 2
                    ♣ A K 4 3
```

South	West	North	East
K. Wei	Ting	Deng	X . . .
—	—	—	2♠
Dble	3♡(!)	No	No
No			

North led the queen of clubs and followed with a trump. The declarer took the last three tricks, in diamonds; six down.

'You tried to bluff me, Ting', said Deng.

'And I succeeded', Ting replied. 'You had game in hearts.'

'Again you are trying to bluff me. You know quite well that over 3NT or four hearts you would have bid four spades.'

'True, and you would have scored the same 300.'

'Wrong', declared Deng, who was accustomed to have the last word. 'Defending against 3♡, we score 300 + 100 honours!'

Marks: Double, 100; pass, 80; three spades, 70; 3NT, 60. (17 votes for double, 5 for pass, 4 for 3♠, 1 for 4♡ or 3NT.)

Point to note: It cannot be far wrong, especially at rubber bridge, to accept a good penalty when you know the opponents have a better spot.

T.R. adds: Sorry, but I still think my 3NT is best! Not knowing how strong you are, they may not sacrifice.

[35]

Mortal Cue-bid

Teams, E–W vulnerable, the bidding goes:

South	West	North	East
—	—	—	1♠
No	No	2♠	Dble
No	No	4♠	No
?			

What should South call, holding:

        ♠ K J 10 7 5 3 2
        ♡ 10 8
        ♢ 9 4 2
        ♣ 7

The nerves of the jury were stretched on this occasion, because they had suffered some shocks in earlier problems.

MOLLO, terrified: 5♢. Is North the same player as in the last question?

DOUCHON: 5♢. Am I playing with an idiot, a half-wit, or a madman?

MEILLAUD: 5♢. This month, for sure, you have given us a partner who is a member of a bloodthirsty commando.

That goes a bit far, for North was none other than the 1976 world champion, Fred Hamilton. He made this four-spade bid during the 1981 American team championship, and if one is to reproach him at all it is for placing too much pressure on his partner. Solodar passed four spades, which went one down. He had only one supporter among the panel:

CALABRO: Pass. Funny chap, North, he has found the perfect contract.

But SAINTE-MARIE saw it differently: 5♢, we won't make four spades.

Why do you suppose that North has lost so much space in

jumping to four spades? This is how DELMOULY answered:

North is a player who likes to torment his partners. This is how I understand his manoeuvres:

(1) He doesn't want to play in four spades since he has removed two spades doubled.
(2) He doesn't want to play in four hearts because he has gone beyond that level.
(3) I conclude, therefore, that he has a very powerful 5-5 or 6-5 minor two-suiter.

So I am tempted to bid six diamonds, but the distribution is sure to be bad (West a singleton spade at most), so I will settle for five diamonds.

PARIENTE saw it the same way: 5◇, but with the queen of diamonds I would bid six.

No-one ventured six diamonds, which would probably have failed, North holding:

♠ —
♡ A 3
◇ A K 10 8 3
♣ A K Q 5 4 2

Perhaps, as TINTNER suggested, North should have bid 4NT instead of four spades, to be absolutely sure that South would not pass.

Marks: Five diamonds, 100; 4NT, 70; pass, 40. (21 votes for 5◇, 4 for 4NT, 1 for pass.)

Point to remember: When your partner makes a very unexpected call, work out what he is trying to say and do not cross his intentions.

Balm on My Heart

At game all the bidding goes:

South	West	North	East
—	—	1♡	No
1NT	No	3♡	No
?			

What should South call, holding:

♠ A J 6
♡ 9
◇ A 7 6 3 2
♣ 10 9 8 7

This problem is one of my saddest memories. It cost me the first prize in the 1960 bidding competition organised by the *Libre Belgique*. My answer was 3NT and my comment: What else can one bid with only a singleton heart? Three spades would indicate only a three-card suit, but would it not imply the lack of a stopper in either diamonds or clubs? True, there are two aces, but is that any reason to bid four hearts and hear partner say: 'Since when does one raise on a singleton? In future, please don't call my hand for me, I'm big enough to rebid four hearts on my own . . .'

Nevertheless, the majority chose four hearts, apparently agreeing with BESSE, who wrote: 4♡. When the main strength of the hand lies in two aces it is generally right to play in the suit.

The vote then was: 8 for four hearts, 3 for 3NT, 1 for three spades.

This result stuck in my throat for twenty years until I put the same problem to the panel of *Le Bridgeur*. Perhaps a change by now? And there was! A distinct majority for 3NT, with three spades well in the running.

MONK: 3NT. Not my style to bid four hearts with a singleton.

MEILLAUD: 3NT. At one time I would have said four hearts. Age, no doubt . . .

And perhaps experience?

There were several votes for three spades, leaving partner the choice between 3NT and four hearts.

DELMOULY: 3♠. Obviously we are going to game, and three spades gives partner a little extra information.

CHEMLA: 3♠. Showing that South, like the donkey in the fable, is unable to choose between 3NT and four hearts.

The donkey, you may remember, was unable to make up its mind which way to go at the crossroads and eventually fell dead between the shafts.

FORQUET and FRENDO: 3♠, indicating useful spades and a maximum for the 1NT response.

Marks: Three spades or 3NT, 100; four hearts, 80; pass, 30; four diamonds, 20. (11 votes for 3NT, 8 for 4♡, 7 for 3♠, 1 for pass.)

Point to remember: After 1♡-1NT-3♡ a bid of three spades by the responder shows values, but fewer than four cards. Also, a jump rebid by the opener shows a strong suit, but this is no reason to support it with a singleton or a low doubleton.

T.R. adds: I have given José his head here, but I am not on his side. After 1♡-1NT-3♡ it seems to me that 3NT would suggest a hand more of this type: K J x Q x J 10 x x Q x x x. With *aces* you should support partner's suit (see Besse's answer). A singleton in his suit may make 3NT unsound.

PART II

Leads and Defence

Where It All Began

Suit preference signals are now an established part of the game, familiar to all players who have passed the learner's stage. Do you know where they began? In August 1934 Hy Lavinthal, a bridge teacher from Trenton (New Jersey), described the following deal in *Le Monde Du Bridge*:

```
                    ♠ K 6
                    ♡ Q 10 8 6 5
                    ◇ 10 4 2
                    ♣ Q J 10
  ♠ A 10 9 7 3 2                    ♠ J 8 5 4
  ♡ —              N                 ♡ 2
  ◇ 9 8 7       W     E              ◇ K 6 5
  ♣ 8 6 5 2        S                 ♣ A 9 7 4 3
                    ♠ Q
                    ♡ A K J 9 7 4 3
                    ◇ A Q J 3
                    ♣ K
```

E–W vulnerable, the bidding went:

South	West	North	East
1♡	1♠	2♡	2♠
6♡	No	No	No

Blackwood was only just born in those happy days!

West led the ace of spades and East perhaps dropped the 5, to show an even number. With no indication, West followed with a low diamond. South's king of clubs went away on the king of spades.

Playing suit preference, of course, East would have dropped the 4 of spades to request a switch to clubs, the jack to ask for a diamond.

Point to remember: On occasions like this, where there could be no possible reason for a spade continuation, the high or low card is a suit preference signal, known more often nowadays as a McKenney.

Resounding Echo

In defence it is usually right to enlighten partner, but there are times when it is still more important to keep the declarer in the dark. This is an area of the game that is seldom discussed, but at rubber bridge, especially, it determines the fate of many contracts.

Here is a typical example. To make his contract of 3NT, the declarer had to divine the position of the ace of spades. West signalled emphatically with the 8 and 6 to show that he held this vital entry card. It was a fatal move, as you will see.

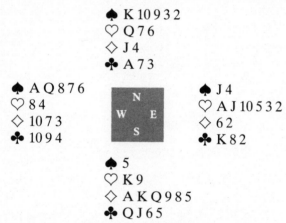

```
                  ♠ K 10 9 3 2
                  ♡ Q 7 6
                  ◇ J 4
                  ♣ A 7 3
  ♠ A Q 8 7 6                      ♠ J 4
  ♡ 8 4              N             ♡ A J 10 5 3 2
  ◇ 10 7 3       W     E          ◇ 6 2
  ♣ 10 9 4          S             ♣ K 8 2
                  ♠ 5
                  ♡ K 9
                  ◇ A K Q 9 8 5
                  ♣ Q J 6 5
```

Dealer South, E–W vulnerable. The bidding went:

South	West	North	East
Le Dentu	P. Dupont	Médan	Catzeflis
1◇	No	1♠	2♡
3◇	No	3♡	No
3NT	No	No	No

North's three hearts was a normal move, asking partner to bid 3NT if he held an honour in hearts. Failing that, South might be able to show delayed support in spades.

West's lead of the 8 of hearts ran to the 10 and king. How should South play now? When I first published this deal, I asked a supplementary question: was West's spade signal an error of judgement, a serious fault, or a monstrous crime?

As is usually the case in 3NT when there are eight tricks in sight, the first play was to cash the long suit. On the fourth and fifth diamonds West signalled with 8 and 6 of spades. After the last diamond the position was:

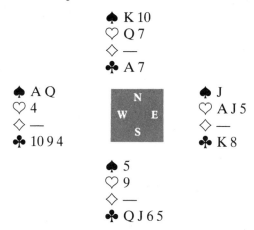

I led a spade now and the defence could take only four tricks.

One must say that West's spade discards were, at the least, a serious error of judgement. His partner *had* to place him with the ace of spades, so there was no point in telling the world about it.

The professional defence on this type of hand would be for East to discard two low *clubs* early on and West to make no signal in spades.

Point to remember: It is normal to signal information to partner about high cards and distribution, but there are many occasions when it is still more important not to assist the declarer.

Forced Card at Venice

As at all games, there are times when the best players in the world are not in form. This was the case at Venice in 1974 when the French team of Boulenger, Svarc, Lebel and Mari failed to reach the semi-final stage of the Bermuda Bowl. True, there was no third pair, and foreign journalists often said to me: 'Why only a team of four? It seems a strange conceit in a country that has so many top-class players.'

And indeed, experience has shown that to field anything less than a team of six (the maximum) is a bad mistake. Perhaps a full team would not have made much difference on this occasion. Here is one deal where the French were victims of the famous Brazilian, Gabriel Chagas. With North–South vulnerable the bidding went:

South	West	North	East
Mari	Chagas	Lebel	Assumpçao
No	No	1♣	4♡
4♠	5♡	No	No
6♣	6♡	6♠	No
No	Dble	all pass	

West, on lead, held:

♠ 10 9 8 3
♡ Q 10 9 7
♢ K Q 7 4 2
♣ —

Which card would you choose? A heart lead would be safe, but the opponents are ready for this and one of them may be void. The danger of leading a trump is that the declarer may be able to draw trumps and run the clubs, perhaps discarding a losing diamond. Best, then, to lead a diamond, but which one?

Your convention is to lead the king from K Q, but here you

would like your partner to win the trick and return a club for you to ruff. So the *queen* of diamonds stands out, and this was the Brazilian's choice.

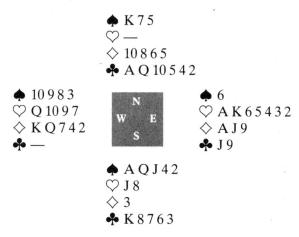

                        ♠ K 7 5
                        ♡ —
                        ◇ 10 8 6 5
                        ♣ A Q 10 5 4 2

        ♠ 10 9 8 3   ♠ 6
        ♡ Q 10 9 7   ♡ A K 6 5 4 3 2
        ◇ K Q 7 4 2   ◇ A J 9
        ♣ —   ♣ J 9

                        ♠ A Q J 4 2
                        ♡ J 8
                        ◇ 3
                        ♣ K 8 7 6 3

It wasn't difficult for East, after this 'impossible' lead of the queen, to overtake and give his partner the club ruff. (Maybe East would have done this even if West had led the king, but that's not quite the point.)

This was the bidding at the other table:

South	West	North	East
Fonseca	Boulenger	Cintra	Svarc
1♠	No	4♠	5♡
No	No	No	

East made twelve tricks after a spade lead, so France still gained on the board.

When this deal was played in the match between Italy and Indonesia, the Italians had a spectacular success: six spades by Belladonna at one table, six hearts, with an overtrick, by Franco at the other.

Point to remember: When you want your partner to capture the first trick, lead the lower of touching honours—the queen from K Q.

Putting It All Together

Good opening leads are the product of good reasoning. Consider this example from the pairs Olympiad at New Orleans in 1978. The French player, Jean-Marc Roudinesco, held the West cards and North–South were vulnerable. The bidding went:

South	West	North	East
Mari	Roudinesco	Perron	Stoppa
—	No	No	1♠
3NT	4♣	No	No
4NT	No	No	No

West held:

♠ Q J 6
♡ A
♢ 4 2
♣ J 10 9 7 5 3 2

The declarer, Christian Mari, has always had the reputation of being a very sound player, not given to flights of fancy. If he bids 3NT, and follows with 4NT, it is reasonable to suppose that he expects to make ten tricks.

Roudi placed him, initially, with seven or eight sure winners in diamonds (or possibly A K of spades and a diamond suit headed by K Q J). He would surely hold at least one guard in spades and presumably at least one guard in clubs.

What about East? He has opened one spade and is unlikely to hold much in either minor suit. He may well hold a second suit of hearts.

Conclusion: the most likely suit for defensive tricks was hearts. The best plan might be to cash the ace of hearts and hope to find partner with a quick entry. So West began with the ace of hearts, and this was the full deal:

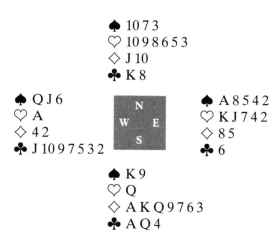

```
              ♠ 10 7 3
              ♡ 10 9 8 6 5 3
              ◇ J 10
              ♣ K 8
♠ Q J 6                        ♠ A 8 5 4 2
♡ A              N             ♡ K J 7 4 2
◇ 4 2        W       E         ◇ 8 5
♣ J 10 9 7 5 3 2     S         ♣ 6
              ♠ K 9
              ♡ Q
              ◇ A K Q 9 7 6 3
              ♣ A Q 4
```

East naturally played the 7 of hearts on the first trick, to confirm that his quick entry card lay in spades. Then a spade switch won four tricks for the defence.

On any other lead, as you can see, the declarer can take at least eleven tricks. This is what happened at several tables.

Point to remember: When wondering what to lead, it is often a good plan to attempt to reconstruct at least one of the other three hands. As a rule, it is easier to picture the declarer's hand than that of partner or the dummy.

Revenge for the Lords

The annual match between the Lords and the Commons, promoted by Rixi Markus, has always had an unusual formula: the cards are duplicated, but the players compete as though they were playing rubber bridge. When a side makes its second game the scores are added, with points for the rubber, and the game starts anew.

In 1979 the Lords were favourites because of the recent ennoblement of Harold Lever, the most experienced player on either side. The issue was in doubt, nevertheless, till a few boards from the finish when the Duke of Atholl found a killing lead against a contract of four spades redoubled. The bidding:

South	West	North	East
Berry	Atholl	Kitson	Birkenhead
—	—	1♡	No
1♠	No	2♡	No
2♠	No	3♣	No
3♠	No	4♠	No
No	Dble	No	No
Redble	No	No	No

West had to find a lead from:

♠ K 10 8 3 2   ♡ 9 6 3   ◇ K Q 9 3   ♣ A

The king of diamonds looks to be a safe lead that would commend itself to most average players, but the Duke took note that North had bid hearts and clubs and had supported spades, so was marked with a singleton diamond.

So what else? The ace of clubs might not be fatal, but it would scarcely gain anything. There seemed little point in a heart through dummy's first suit. No, a trump was indicated. It might cost a trick early on, but it would surely prevent one of the diamond ruffs in dummy. Also, when a defender hoards a long trump holding he is liable to be strangled at the finish.

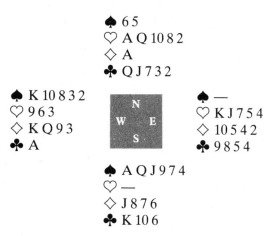

After the trump lead South had to lose two spades, a diamond and a club.

Much the same after a diamond lead, do you think? Not necessarily. Imagine this sequence of play: ace of diamonds, ace of hearts (South discarding a diamond) and heart ruff, diamond ruff, heart ruff, diamond ruff.

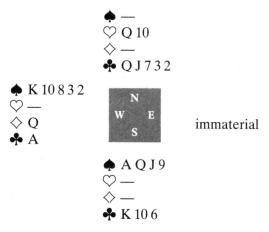

immaterial

The declarer exits with a club and cannot be prevented from making four more tricks in spades.

Point to remember: When you know that the dummy holds trumps and a short side suit, lead a trump.

The Four Madonnas

Ida, Alma, Adriana and Titsiana—four delightful forenames
that you would find only in Italy. These four were the heroines
of a remarkable event in 1987. First, suppose that in a friendly
game of rubber bridge you had to find a lead after this
sequence:

South	West	North	East
Pellegri	Cova	Mazzadi	Saleti
1♣	5♣	Dble	No
5♠	No	6♠	7♣
7♠	No	No	No

The opening one club was strong and conventional. West's
five clubs was weak and (you may think) diabolical. North's
double was of the negative type, showing values. Now West
has to lead against seven spades from:

♠ 8 7 2
♡ 9 6 2
◇ —
♣ Q 10 8 7 5 3 2

When Ida Pellegri, the Italian journalist, asked me what I
would have led from the West hand I answered 'a trump'. This
could hardly cost a trick and might prevent one of the ruffs in
the North hand.

A trump lead would indeed have been effective, but it
would have spoilt a marvellous story. West in practice led a
club and Ida's singleton 2 of diamonds turned out to be the
most beautiful card she had held in her life. This was the full
deal:

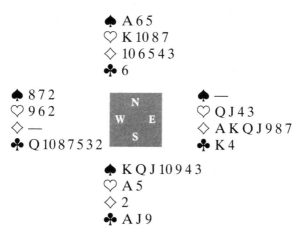

                    ♠ A 6 5
                    ♡ K 10 8 7
                    ◇ 10 6 5 4 3
                    ♣ 6

♠ 8 7 2   ♠ —
♡ 9 6 2   N   ♡ Q J 4 3
◇ —   W   E   ◇ A K Q J 9 8 7
♣ Q 10 8 7 5 3 2   S   ♣ K 4

                    ♠ K Q J 10 9 4 3
                    ♡ A 5
                    ◇ 2
                    ♣ A J 9

After the club lead South ruffed a club, returned to hand
with a trump, and ruffed another club. She regained the lead
♡A and led the remaining trumps, arriving at this position:

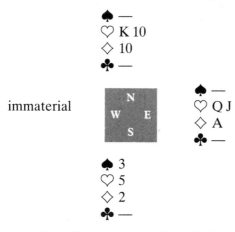

                    ♠ —
                    ♡ K 10
                    ◇ 10
                    ♣ —

                                    ♠ —
immaterial   N   ♡ Q J
              W   E   ◇ A
                   S   ♣ —

                    ♠ 3
                    ♡ 5
                    ◇ 2
                    ♣ —

Dummy's 10 of diamonds was discarded on the last trump
and East could only ask for a stay of execution.

Point to remember: Against a grand slam a trump lead can
hardly cost and may create a small entry problem for the
declarer.

A Precaution that Costs Nothing

There are musical prodigies, and chess prodigies, and even, in these times, tennis prodigies, but few, if any, child prodigies at bridge. It is too many-sided a game. But from the age of 21 or so you may come across some excellent play. Look at this slam contract, played by the Norwegian Stoevneng during the European Junior Championship at Budapest in 1986.

West, the opening leader, held:

♠ K 73   ♡ J 10 9 6   ◇ 8 3 2   ♣ 9 6 2

I will spare you the interminable auction that led to a contract of six hearts by South. Suffice it to say that South, Stoevneng, had bid hearts twice and clubs, and North, Vol, had bid diamonds and spades. Some players might have led a spade through dummy's suit, but it is just as sensible to begin with a trump. Would you, therefore, have made the same choice as the Belgian defender—the jack of hearts?

The full hand turns out to be:

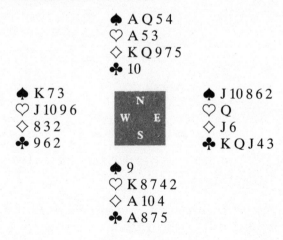

```
                    ♠ A Q 5 4
                    ♡ A 5 3
                    ◇ K Q 9 7 5
                    ♣ 10
  ♠ K 7 3                           ♠ J 10 8 6 2
  ♡ J 10 9 6          N             ♡ Q
  ◇ 8 3 2         W       E         ◇ J 6
  ♣ 9 6 2             S             ♣ K Q J 4 3
                    ♠ 9
                    ♡ K 8 7 4 2
                    ◇ A 10 4
                    ♣ A 8 7 5
```

The declarer won with the ace of hearts in dummy and noted the fall of the queen from East. What did this suggest? Q 10 doubleton? No, West would not have led the jack of trumps from J 9 x. Q 10 9? Unlikely that West would have led the jack from J x. It was far more likely that the queen was a singleton.

In this case the only chance would lie in an elimination and an endplay against West. Stoevneng proceeded as follows: ace of hearts, club to ace, club ruff, diamond to the ace, spade finesse (essential); ace of spades, discarding diamond, spade ruff, club ruff with dummy's last trump. Now the K Q of diamonds stand up and the last three cards are:

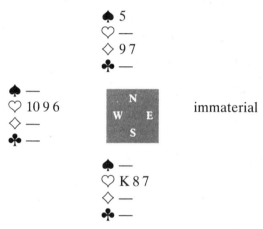

It's all over. 'Well played—nothing we could do', says West. But there was! He should have led the *ten* of hearts, not the jack. Then South would probably have played East for Q J alone or Q J 9 rather than attempt a hazardous trump coup.

Point to remember: When it won't matter if you deceive your partner, deceive the opponent.

A Double Sheds Light

In the galaxy of doubles will there ever be a time when none are left to discover—not even in a black hole? Once, in an encyclopaedia, I listed about ten different types of double, but sometimes the distinction between one and another is not altogether clear. However, in the field of take-out doubles, it is generally possible, with a little intelligence, to perceive what partner is trying to say. Put yourself in the position of Jean-Paul Meyer on this deal from the French team championship in 1986. Sitting West, he held:

♠ K 8 4
♡ A 6
♢ 8 6 5 3
♣ 7 6 5 4

At game all the bidding had been:

South	West	North	East
Tissot	Meyer	Mari	Le Royer
—	—	1♢	No
1♡	No	2♡	Dble
4♡	No	No	No

What was the meaning of East's double of two hearts after he had passed over one diamond? It had to mean that he had values in the two unbid suits, spades and clubs.

What is the best lead, then? The fact that East passed on the first round, though evidently holding fair values, makes it unlikely that his main shortage is in diamonds; he is far more likely to hold a singleton heart.

There is nothing to recommend a trump lead, so the choice must be between spades and clubs. A spade looks a better prospect, partly because you hold a high honour and partly because you have only three spades.

But which spade? A low card is normal from K x x, but Meyer led the king, and this turned out to be a brilliant choice.

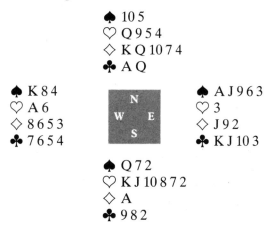

```
                    ♠ 10 5
                    ♡ Q 9 5 4
                    ◇ K Q 10 7 4
                    ♣ A Q
    ♠ K 8 4                         ♠ A J 9 6 3
    ♡ A 6            N              ♡ 3
    ◇ 8 6 5 3     W     E           ◇ J 9 2
    ♣ 7 6 5 4        S              ♣ K J 10 3
                    ♠ Q 7 2
                    ♡ K J 10 8 7 2
                    ◇ A
                    ♣ 9 8 2
```

When the king of spades held the first trick, Meyer switched to a club. There was nothing the declarer could do now. If he goes up with the ace of clubs and crosses to the ace of diamonds, he cannot return quickly to the table to take discards on the K Q of diamonds.

Did it seem to you for a moment that a low spade lead would have worked just as well? No, this was the lead at the other table. The defence took the ace and king of spades and West switched to a club; now South went up with the ace of clubs, crossed to the ace of diamonds, and was able to return to dummy by ruffing the third round of spades.

Point to remember: While the standard lead from K x x of a side suit is the low card, it is good play to lead the king when there is a chance that you can hold the trick and reserve the option of switching to another suit.

Compare the Old and the New

Nobody could deny that modern bidding is superior to that of the early days, but in the play of the cards are the moderns better than those of the pre-war years? Certainly there are many more good players, but are they any better than such as Karl Schneider and Hans Jellinek, the stars of the Austrian team in the 1930s?

Consider Jellinek's play as East on the following deal:

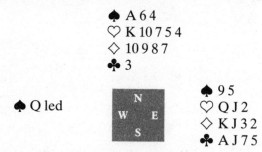

```
              ♠ A 6 4
              ♡ K 10 7 5 4
              ◇ 10 9 8 7
              ♣ 3
                                    ♠ 9 5
                          N         ♡ Q J 2
  ♠ Q led        W            E     ◇ K J 3 2
                          S         ♣ A J 7 5
```

The bidding was on the following lines:

South	West	North	East
1NT	No	2♡	No
3◇	No	4◇	No
5◇	No	No	No

In the Culbertson system the suit response over 1NT was forcing for one round. The Stayman convention came much later.

West led the queen of spades, won by dummy's ace. A club was won by East, who returned a spade to South's king. The declarer discarded a spade from dummy on the king of clubs and ruffed a spade with the 7 of diamonds. How do you suppose that the play went from this point?

Well, Jellinek overruffed with the *king*. You can see the effect of that when you look at the full hand.

[58]

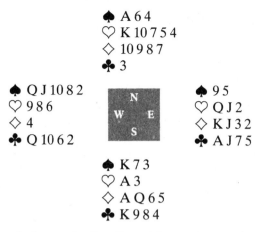

♠ A 6 4
♡ K 10 7 5 4
♢ 10 9 8 7
♣ 3

♠ Q J 10 8 2
♡ 9 8 6
♢ 4
♣ Q 10 6 2

♠ 9 5
♡ Q J 2
♢ K J 3 2
♣ A J 7 5

♠ K 7 3
♡ A 3
♢ A Q 6 5
♣ K 9 8 4

To remind you, the first five tricks were: ace of spades, club to ace, spade to king, discard of a spade on club king, spade ruffed by the 7 of diamonds. Jellinek overruffed with the king, and now, inevitably, South played off the ace and queen of diamonds when he regained the lead. One can imagine his feelings when West showed out on the second round: disappointment, mixed with admiration.

Point to remember: When in defence you hold K J x x of the trump suit, an overruff of the king may be the means of your taking a trick with the jack later on.

T.R. adds: This particular stratagem is fairly well known nowadays, though I doubt whether the opportunity often occurs.

The captain of the great Austrian team, Paul Stern, escaped to England before the war began. It was his amiable practice, whenever he thought of a brilliant play, to attribute it to one of his former players, so much so that the phrase 'Schneider played it' entered the language. So, it is just possible that this story is not absolutely true!

The Only Chance

In the world championship at Buenos Aires in 1961 one of the most interesting deals from a defensive point of view was no. 124 of France's match against the Argentine. The heart game would have been defeated if Ricardo Calvente had analysed the problem in the way that Garozzo, Belladonna or Forquet would surely have done.

♠ A K 10
♡ 9 8 4
◇ 8 7 6
♣ A J 8 7

◇ A led

♠ Q 6 5
♡ 10 5
◇ K J 10 5 3
♣ K 9 3

With North–South vulnerable the bidding went:

South	West	North	East
Le Dentu	Rocchi	Trézel	Calvente
—	—	1♣	1◇
1♠	No	2♠	No
3♡	No	4♡	No
No	No		

North–South were playing *canapé*, which meant here that South's hearts would be at least as long as his spades.

West began with ace and another diamond. South ruffed the third round and played three top hearts, West dropping the jack on the third round. Declarer then crossed to the ace of spades and led a low club from the dummy. East went in with the king and South played low. The question is, what should East play now?

It is essential to reconstruct the South hand. He is known to hold five hearts to the A K Q and a doubleton diamond. He surely has four spades (he bid them) and no doubt he started with Q x of clubs. The whole hand is clear:

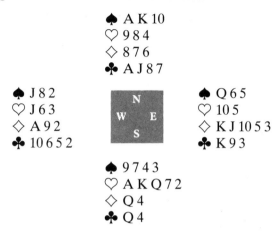

♠ A K 10
♡ 9 8 4
◇ 8 7 6
♣ A J 8 7

♠ J 8 2   ♠ Q 6 5
♡ J 6 3   ♡ 10 5
◇ A 9 2   ◇ K J 10 5 3
♣ 10 6 5 2   ♣ K 9 3

♠ 9 7 4 3
♡ A K Q 7 2
◇ Q 4
♣ Q 4

(My response of one spade looks pretty horrible, but it was safe enough when playing the *canapé* style and it might deter the opponents from leading the suit.)

When East won with the king of clubs he should have realised that a diamond (or club) return would allow the declarer to cash the queen of clubs, cross to the king of spades and make two more club tricks. The only chance was to play partner for the jack of spades. When the jack forces dummy's king the declarer will lack the entries to cash three club tricks.

Point to remember: If there is a chance to defeat a contract, take it, however small it may seem.

Who Is Fooling Whom?

We are not thinking here of the famous phrase of Basil in *The Barber of Seville*, but of the question that every defender should ask himself when he decides to play a deceptive card.

The following deal is a famous example of this hazard. It occurred during the semi-final of the Olympiad at Deauville in 1968 and assisted the Americans to defeat the Dutch and reach the final.

```
              ♠ A K 10 8 7 4
              ♡ 10 6 5
              ◇ —
              ♣ K J 10 4
  ♠ 3 2
  ♡ A 8 7 4 3
  ◇ 10 6 4 3
  ♣ 7 3
```

South was the dealer and East–West were vulnerable. The bidding went:

South	West	North	East
Robinson	Kokkes	Jordan	Heusden
1♡	No	1♠	No
3◇	No	3♠	No
3NT	No	6♡	No
No	No		

West led the 7 of clubs, followed by the 4 from dummy, the 2 from East and the ace from South. A low diamond was ruffed, East dropping the 9 (to show four). The 10 of hearts held the next trick, then a heart ran to the ace, East discarding the 5 and 6 of clubs. After winning this second heart, what should West play next?

It wasn't difficult for Kokkes to construct the deal. He could place his partner with a void in hearts, four diamonds, and five low clubs. The best defence at this point, obviously, was to remove dummy's spade entry. It would then be inconvenient for the declarer to leave the dummy: he would have to play a club to the queen (to draw trumps) and would then be cut off from the remaining winners on the table.

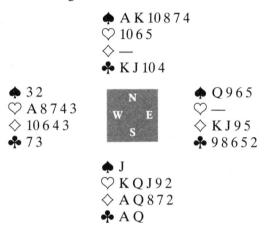

```
                    ♠ A K 10 8 7 4
                    ♡ 10 6 5
                    ◇ —
                    ♣ K J 10 4
  ♠ 3 2                              ♠ Q 9 6 5
  ♡ A 8 7 4 3          N            ♡ —
  ◇ 10 6 4 3       W       E        ◇ K J 9 5
  ♣ 7 3                S             ♣ 9 8 6 5 2
                    ♠ J
                    ♡ K Q J 9 2
                    ◇ A Q 8 7 2
                    ♣ A Q
```

Having reached this conclusion—that a spade was necessary—Kokkes relaxed for a moment and advanced the 2 of spades. Robinson saw quickly that his only chance was to win this trick in his own hand, so he played low from dummy; and now Heusden, assuming too readily that his partner had led the 2 of spades from J 3 2, inserted the 9! It was then simple for the declarer to draw trumps and overtake the queen of clubs.

At the other table the great Dutch player, Bobby Slavenburg, was one down in the same contract. He confided to me later that he was not altogether pleased with the '2 and 9 of spades played by his . . . very dear friends.'

Point to remember: Don't try to deceive your opponent when it may be dangerous to deceive your partner.

The Bermuda Triangle

By winning the European Championship in Israel in 1975, the French team qualified for the world championship in Bermuda. Among their opponents were the Italian Blue Team, which included Belladonna and Garozzo, and the American team known as the Dallas Aces, which included Hamman and Wolff.

The result was a great disappointment for the French, who lost to the Americans in the semi-final after beating them twice in the preliminary rounds.

This deal from the second qualifying round illustrates a point which has never been properly defined.

At game all the bidding went:

South	West	North	East
Swanson	Lebel	Soloway	Mari
1NT	No	3NT	No
No	No		

West led the 4 of clubs (fourth best) to the 8, ace and jack. When East returned the 9 of clubs South played the queen and West the 3. South then advanced the king of spades. Two questions arise:

1. Should East win at once with the ace of spades?

2. If he does win with the ace of spades, what should he play next?

Well, the first question is easy: certainly you must take the ace of spades, because no doubt the diamonds are solid and if you let the king of spades win the declarer will run nine tricks (six diamonds, one spade, one club that you know of, and either ace of hearts or king of clubs).

The second question is not so easy: should you return a club, where partner may hold five to the king, or should you try a heart?

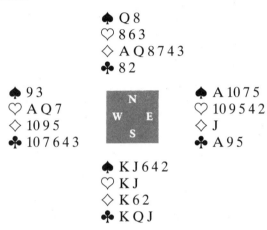

```
              ♠ Q 8
              ♡ 8 6 3
              ◇ A Q 8 7 4 3
              ♣ 8 2
♠ 9 3                          ♠ A 10 7 5
♡ A Q 7                        ♡ 10 9 5 4 2
◇ 10 9 5                       ◇ J
♣ 10 7 6 4 3                   ♣ A 9 5
              ♠ K J 6 4 2
              ♡ K J
              ◇ K 6 2
              ♣ K Q J
```

Mari worked it out like this: if my partner had held K x x x x in clubs he would have dropped a high club on the second round, to encourage a club return. So, despite the fact that his hearts were moderate, Mari led a low heart at trick four and took five tricks in this suit.

At the other table Svarc, in the same contract of 3NT, tried the effect of cashing six diamonds early on. The defenders kept the right cards and he was one down. It was still a gain of 5 IMP to France.

Point to remember: When you have led fourth best from a five-card suit, drop an encouraging card on the second round if you want to impress on partner that this is the suit to play, a low card when you want him to try something else.

Queen Sacrifice

Argine, an anagram of Regina, is a name that French players often use for the queen of clubs. This card was destined to be the heroine of a defence that I recall with special pleasure. These were the hands of North and West:

♠ K J 5
♡ A K Q 10 4
◇ A 8 7
♣ 5 4

♠ Q 3
♡ 6 5 2
◇ J 9
♣ A K J 10 9 6

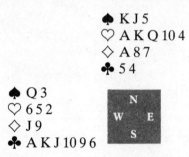

North–South were vulnerable and the bidding went:

South	West	North	East
Y. Lamielle	N. Gallet	Lefébure	Le Dentu
—	1♣	Dble	1♡
1♠	2♣	3♣	Dble
4♠	No	No	No

Nicole Gallet led the king of clubs, on which East played the queen (Argine) and South the 2.

What did that mean? It is usual to play the queen from Q J when partner has led the king. Obviously, East did not hold Q J. The queen may also be played if a singleton, but West recalled that her partner had doubled North's cue-bid of three clubs.

Judging that in any event the queen could not be a discouraging card, Nicole continued with the ace of clubs and a third round. This was excellent for our team, because the full hand was:

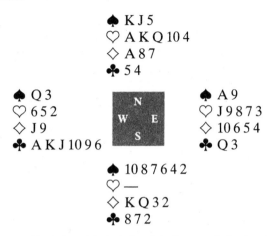

```
              ♠ K J 5
              ♡ A K Q 10 4
              ◇ A 8 7
              ♣ 5 4
♠ Q 3                      ♠ A 9
♡ 6 5 2        N          ♡ J 9 8 7 3
◇ J 9        W   E        ◇ 10 6 5 4
♣ A K J 10 9 6   S        ♣ Q 3
              ♠ 10 8 7 6 4 2
              ♡ —
              ◇ K Q 3 2
              ♣ 8 7 2
```

South ruffed the third club with dummy's jack of spades. I declined, on general principles, to overruff, and from this point the defence was sure to make two trump tricks, defeating the contract.

You will see that if I had overruffed the jack of spades with the ace, South might have led the 10 on the next round, pinning the 9.

Point to remember: Refusing to overruff will often gain a trick in an unexpected way. I came across this position recently:

```
              Q
       A 6 4     K 10
          J 9 8 7 5 3 2
```

South at one point ruffed a side suit with dummy's queen of trumps and East overruffed. When he gained the lead South advanced the jack of trumps and lost only one more trick. But if East had declined to overruff the queen . . .

[67]

The Three Swiss

Switzerland, like France, has its Three Musketeers. They are Jean Besse, Pietro Bernasconi, and Jimmy Ortiz-Patino, who for many years was President of the World Bridge Federation.

These three, with support that was constantly changing, were always a threat to the leading teams. They had their best run in the 1964 Olympiad, when they led their section for eight rounds, not losing until they encountered the strong British team. This was a critical deal in that match:

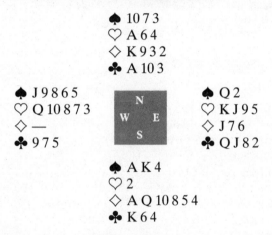

```
              ♠ 10 7 3
              ♡ A 6 4
              ◇ K 9 3 2
              ♣ A 10 3

♠ J 9 8 6 5              ♠ Q 2
♡ Q 10 8 7 3            ♡ K J 9 5
◇ —                     ◇ J 7 6
♣ 9 7 5                 ♣ Q J 8 2

              ♠ A K 4
              ♡ 2
              ◇ A Q 10 8 5 4
              ♣ K 6 4
```

At game all the bidding went:

South	West	North	East
Bernasconi	Schapiro	Ortiz	Reese
1◇	No	3◇	No
3♠	No	3NT	No
4♣	No	4♡	No
6◇	No	No	No

To succeed in this borderline contract, South was probably going to need an elimination play of some kind. He won the heart lead, ruffed a heart, drew three rounds of trumps, and ruffed dummy's last heart. West, meanwhile, had discarded two spades and one heart.

The next card was the ace of spades, and it looks as though Pietro's general plan is going to succeed. If he cashes two spades and follows with three rounds of clubs, East will be left on play, forced to concede a ruff-and-discard.

However, Reese created a variation by dropping the queen of spades under the ace. This could not possibly cost, because it was certain from the bidding and play that the declarer held A K of spades.

After this fall of the queen of spades Bernasconi seemed to have better prospects than before. Indeed, if the queen were singleton, then three rounds of clubs would surely win the contract: either East would win the third club and concede a ruff-and-discard, or West would win and would have to have to lead from the jack of spades. But when South followed this plan, East won the third club and produced an embarrassing 2 of spades.

The deal cost the Swiss 13 match points, because at the other table the British pair stopped in game.

Point to remember: When you hold a doubleton honour, such as K 10 under an opponent's A Q, it can hardly cost to play the king on the first round and may mislead the opponent. This is a standard position:

```
         A Q 6 4 2
  K 10              8 5 3
         J 9 7
```

After the 7 has been headed by the king and ace the declarer may finesse the 9 on the way back.

The Fine Art of Defence

In the course of a long interview for *Le Bridgeur* the great French player, Paul Chemla, expressed this opinion about defensive play and signalling:

'You must have complete understanding with your partner. By complete, I don't mean elaborate. Most players much overdo their signalling systems.* Then the slightest misunderstanding can lead to catastrophe.'

'If you look at the records of big matches played in the 1950s and 60s, you will find that the best players used very few signals indeed. Intelligence and a feeling for the game are all-important. Nothing replaces that.'

Very true, but it should be remembered that the most important signals, relating to strength and distribution, have been in place since the early 1930s.

And Paul, who likes his little joke, went on to say that defence was the easiest part of the game. When the interviewer, Norbert Lebely, remarked that most people found the defence difficult, Chemla replied, 'I have never understood why'.

---

* 'Carding' is the ghastly word used by those players who are always trying to tell the world what they hold. 'Don't give me any signals', Rixi Markus used to say to her shivering partners in an Individual. 'After two or three tricks I'll know what you've got in your hand better than you know yourself.'—T.R.

For most people, playing with a partner whose cards you cannot see is more difficult than playing the dummy. As an example of fine defence, study the play by Mike Kopera, who was West on this deal from a tournament in Lancaster (USA).

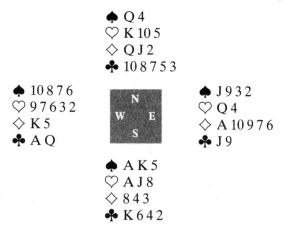

```
                    ♠ Q 4
                    ♡ K 10 5
                    ◇ Q J 2
                    ♣ 10 8 7 5 3
    ♠ 10 8 7 6                      ♠ J 9 3 2
    ♡ 9 7 6 3 2                     ♡ Q 4
    ◇ K 5                           ◇ A 10 9 7 6
    ♣ A Q                           ♣ J 9
                    ♠ A K 5
                    ♡ A J 8
                    ◇ 8 4 3
                    ♣ K 6 4 2
```

South, who had opened 1NT, played in 2NT and West began with a heart to the queen and ace. The declarer led a spade to the queen, then a club to the 9, king and ace.

What do you suppose happened now? Right! West played king and another diamond, then discarded the queen of clubs on the third round. East (Ira Herman) came in with the jack of clubs and made two more diamonds, for one down.

Point to remember: Don't fail to count the declarer's points, especially when he has bid notrumps. Here he was marked with 7 points in spades, 5 in hearts, and 3 in clubs. Since he passed the raise to 2NT, this was likely to be all. True, you still have to think of discarding the queen of clubs!

The Columbus Coup

To discover America, you have to think of it. There is a story that when Christopher Columbus was trying to gain support from a group of distrustful Spanish grandees he asked a servant to bring an egg and said 'Who can make this egg stand upright?'

Nobody could. Columbus then tapped one end on his plate, and the egg obeyed. Said the explorer: 'You see, it's not difficult, but you have to think of it.'

A problem of this sort confronted the defence on a deal from the 1978 Olympiad at New Orleans.

```
                    ♠ 9 8 6
                    ♡ A K Q 7
                    ◇ A 4
                    ♣ 10 9 5 2

   ♠ K 10 4 3
   ♡ J 3
   ◇ 9 5
   ♣ A K Q 8 3
```

With North–South vulnerable, the bidding went:

South	West	North	East
Sharif	N. Cohen	Hussein	Tintner
—	—	1♣	2♠
3♡	4♠	5♡	all pass

Nadine Cohen cashed two clubs, everyone following. Where to go for a third trick? South was surely void in spades. If East held the king of diamonds he would make it in due course.

So Nadine tried a third round of clubs. And her partner held the singleton 10 of hearts. It was enough.

PART III

Declarer's Play

First Victory for France

The first European Championship of Contract Bridge, as it was called then, was played in 1932. In 1932 and 1933 the championship was won by Austria, in 1934 by Hungary. In 1935 France took the field with a team already famous—Albarran, de Nexon, Rousset and Venizelos (a Greek). This team gained a famous victory, winning ten matches out of eleven.

A slam contract made by Albarran against the young Hungarian team decided the issue of a critical match.

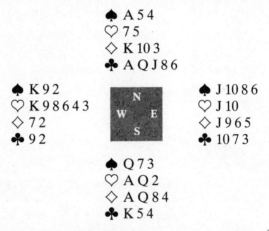

```
                    ♠ A 5 4
                    ♡ 7 5
                    ◇ K 10 3
                    ♣ A Q J 8 6
    ♠ K 9 2                         ♠ J 10 8 6
    ♡ K 9 8 6 4 3       N          ♡ J 10
    ◇ 7 2           W       E      ◇ J 9 6 5
    ♣ 9 2               S          ♣ 10 7 3
                    ♠ Q 7 3
                    ♡ A Q 2
                    ◇ A Q 8 4
                    ♣ K 5 4
```

At game all the bidding went:

South	West	North	East
Albarran	X . .	De Nexon	Y . .
1NT	No	3♣ (1)	No
3♠ (2)	No	4♠	No
4NT (3)	No	5NT	No
6NT	No	No	No

(1) In the absence of any special conventions, this jump in a minor suit was a slam suggestion.

(2) Semi-psychic, designed to avert a possibly dangerous lead.

(3) Natural. The Blackwood convention had been played in America since 1933, but was not yet prevalent in Europe.

West's lead of the 7 of diamonds ran to the 9 and queen. When five rounds of clubs were played, East discarded a heart and a diamond (removing all doubt in this suit). Three more rounds of diamonds led to this ending:

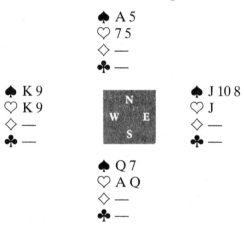

West had signalled in hearts and was quite likely to hold the king of spades, so Albarran played off ace and queen of hearts, making a slam that was not bid at the other table.

Point to remember: West's lead from a doubleton of an unbid suit made this contract easier to play. It was certain that South would have a fair holding in diamonds.

Slender Clue

One of the founders of the European Bridge League, Johannes Brun, of Norway, had to decide whether to look for an extra trick in spades or clubs on this deal from the 1933 championship.

```
              ♠ A K 8 5 3
              ♡ Q 4
              ♢ 2
              ♣ A K 6 5 2
  ♢ K led

              ♠ 4
              ♡ K J 10 7 5 2
              ♢ J 7 6 4 3
              ♣ 4
```

With North–South vulnerable the bidding had been:

South	West	North	East
—	—	1♣	No
1♡	2♢	2♠	No
3♡	No	4♡	No
No	No		

West led the king of diamonds, on which East's queen appeared, then switched to a trump. East won with the ace and played a second round, won by South's king. On the next heart West discarded a diamond and the declarer had to decide whether to throw a spade or a club from dummy. Would it matter, and if so, which was right?

If you count the tricks you will see that South has nine tricks on top and will need to establish a long card in one or other of the black suits. Even then, it looks as though he will be an entry short to the dummy.

There was just one indication: with five spades, ace of hearts, and queen of diamonds (these are known), East might have overcalled the opening one diamond. Taking note of this slender clue, Brun discarded a club from dummy. Still short of an entry? No, look at the full hand:

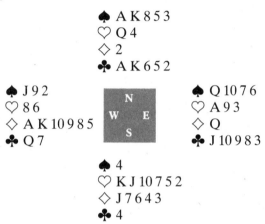

```
              ♠ A K 8 5 3
              ♡ Q 4
              ♢ 2
              ♣ A K 6 5 2

♠ J 9 2                        ♠ Q 10 7 6
♡ 8 6                          ♡ A 9 3
♢ A K 10 9 8 5                 ♢ Q
♣ Q 7                          ♣ J 10 9 8 3

              ♠ 4
              ♡ K J 10 7 5 2
              ♢ J 7 6 4 3
              ♣ 4
```

After discarding a club from dummy on the third round of trumps, South played three rounds of spades, ruffing, then a club to the ace and a fourth spade on which he discarded a diamond. East had to win and, with only clubs left, had to return a club to dummy's king. The long spade was the declarer's tenth trick.

Point to remember: You must take note of any bids made by the defending side—but also of any bid that was *not* made!

March of Time

In 1937 the recently created World Bridge Federation organised at Budapest the first world championship. Culbertson brought two teams from America that played his system. In France the Albarran team that had brilliantly won the European Championship in 1935 was beaten in the French championship by a team that included a young medical student, Pierre Jaïs, then 23. The winners were chosen to represent their country; they finished ninth.*

The final was a dramatic encounter between Culbertson and the Austrians. The match was level for a long way, but Austria finally won by 4,740 (aggregate) points.

How strong were the champions of those days? From among the 96 boards I have found one, especially, that may seem to provide a clue. Frischauer was defeated in a contract of five spades and the experts declared that even a player of his calibre could not gauge the distribution well enough to make eleven tricks.

These were the North–South cards on board 84:

> ♠ K 9
> ♡ 10 3
> ♢ A K 10 8 4
> ♣ Q 6 5 3

♡ A led

> ♠ A J 8 6 5 3 2
> ♡ 4
> ♢ J 6
> ♣ K J 8

North–South were vulnerable and the bidding went:

*It was the old story, still prevalent: so-called selectors fail to *select.*—T.R.

South	West	North	East
Frischauer	*Vogelhofer*	*Herbert*	*H. Sobel*
—	3♡	No	3NT
4♠	5♡	5♠	Dble
No	No	No	

West began with ace and king of hearts. South ruffed and played the king of clubs, won by East, who returned the 10 of clubs. How should South play now?

When you have made your decision, look at the full hand:

♠ K 9
♡ 10 3
♢ A K 10 8 4
♣ Q 6 5 3

♠ —
♡ A K Q J 7 6 2
♢ 9 7 3 2
♣ 7 4

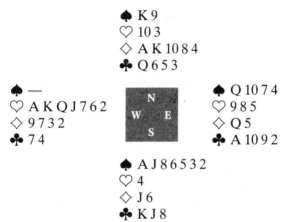

♠ Q 10 7 4
♡ 9 8 5
♢ Q 5
♣ A 10 9 2

♠ A J 8 6 5 3 2
♡ 4
♢ J 6
♣ K J 8

South ruffs the second heart, loses a club to East and wins the return. The winning play now is: club to the queen, spade 9 to the 10 and jack, diamond to ace, fourth club ruffed; diamond to king, diamond ruff, spade to king; the lead is in dummy and South holds ♠ A 8 over East's Q 7.

As the defence was played, a top player today might have made this contract. East was marked with all the trumps and a trump coup was the only way to make eleven tricks.

Point to remember: No doubt most players would have done the same, but the defenders made two small mistakes. From West's angle, South would surely welcome a chance to shorten his trumps, so the second heart was not good play. For the same reason, East's early play of the ace of clubs (if correctly reported) was a mistake.

The Auto Coup

I called this deal the Auto Coup when it was played in 1955 at the famous Automobile Club in Paris. It is instructive in both a psychological and technical sense.

```
              ♠ K 7
              ♡ A 10 8 6 5
              ◇ A Q 5 4
              ♣ 7 6
  ♣ J led

              ♠ A 10 9 8 5 4 3
              ♡ 9 7 3
              ◇ 7
              ♣ A 4
```

At game to North–South the bidding went:

South	West	North	East
—	—	1♡	2♣
2♠	3♣	3♠	4♣
6♠ (!)	No	No	No

After this dynamic auction West led the jack of clubs. South won with the ace, finessed the queen of diamonds successfully and discarded his second club on the ace of diamonds. How should he continue, do you think?

Philippe de Boysson made a surprising play: he led a low heart from the table. See the pressure that this put on East, since the full hand was:

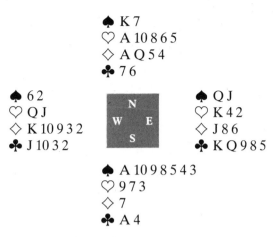

```
              ♠ K 7
              ♡ A 10 8 6 5
              ◇ A Q 5 4
              ♣ 7 6
♠ 6 2                          ♠ Q J
♡ Q J            N             ♡ K 4 2
◇ K 10 9 3 2   W   E           ◇ J 8 6
♣ J 10 3 2       S             ♣ K Q 9 8 5
              ♠ A 10 9 8 5 4 3
              ♡ 9 7 3
              ◇ 7
              ♣ A 4
```

East went up with the king of hearts. End of story.

Admittedly, this was not smart play by East. South might have held something like Q 9 x in hearts. When I showed the deal to the great British player, Adam Meredith, he suggested a different line:

After winning the first trick with the ace of clubs, play six rounds of spades, *discarding three hearts from the table*. It is quite possible that East, who would have to make four discards, would let go a heart. Then queen and ace of diamonds, followed by ace and another heart, would leave South with a trump and a good heart.

Observe that if the opening lead had been a diamond South would not have needed to rely on a mistake by the defence. He finesses the diamond queen, discards a *heart* on the ace of diamonds, then leads a *low* heart. When he wins the next trick with the ace of clubs he plays ace of spades, heart to the ace, heart ruff, and spade to the king. The trumps have been drawn and the hearts are good.

Point to remember: The discarding of three hearts from dummy (in Meredith's play) would cause many defenders to think that you were not interested in this suit.

An Illuminating Discard

Some contracts that look difficult at one point become possible when you have formed a picture of the distribution.

♠ 9 3
♡ A Q J 4
♢ K 6 2
♣ A K 8 2

♠ K led

♠ A 10 6 5
♡ 3
♢ A 10 9 8 7 3
♣ 9 3

North was the dealer and North–South were vulnerable. The bidding by my partner and myself in a mixed pairs was not exactly classical.

South	West	North	East
Le Dentu	Baguenault	Souza Lage	Montaigu
—	—	1♡	No
2♢	No	2NT	No
3♢	No	5♢	No
No	No		

West led the king of spades and I won in hand. Needing one or two spade ruffs, I returned a low spade. West won with the queen and led a third round, ruffed by dummy's 2 of diamonds. I played the king of diamonds next and had a shock when East showed out, discarding a club.

At this point I had to try for an endplay against West, who appeared to have two trump winners. I played ace of hearts and ruffed a heart, then crossed to ♣ K and ruffed another heart, on which West's king fell. How would you assess the position now?

It may look as though West began with 3-3-4-3 distribution. But (a) East's early discard of a club was significant: it strongly suggested that she had begun with five clubs; and (b) I knew that West, Jean Baguenault, was a skilful and imaginative player, quite capable of dropping the king of hearts on the third round to mislead me. At any rate, instead of seeking to shorten my hand with a ruff of the third club, I crossed to ♣ A and led another heart. This turned out to be the right game, for the full hand was:

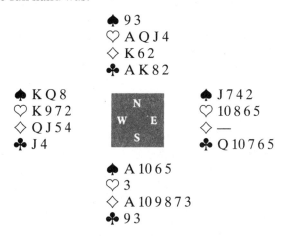

```
              ♠ 9 3
              ♡ A Q J 4
              ◇ K 6 2
              ♣ A K 8 2
♠ K Q 8                    ♠ J 7 4 2
♡ K 9 7 2        N         ♡ 10 8 6 5
◇ Q J 5 4    W     E       ◇ —
♣ J 4            S         ♣ Q 10 7 6 5
              ♠ A 10 6 5
              ♡ 3
              ◇ A 10 9 8 7 3
              ♣ 9 3
```

At the end I was able to lead my fourth spade and West, with Q J 5 of trumps in front of dummy's 6, could only ruff high and concede the last two tricks to my A 10.

Point to remember: When dummy holds four useful cards in a suit (clubs in this instance) and a defender discards in this suit early on, it is generally safe to assume that this player holds five or more.

The First Olympiad

In the spring of 1960 the first Olympiad was played at Turin. There were twenty teams, including four from America, because in those days entry was proportionate to national membership. Italy and Britain were known to be strong, but France had a very well-balanced team, consisting of Jaïs-Trézel, Ghestem-Bacherich, Bourchtoff-Delmouly. The captain, Robert de Nexon, simply fielded his three pairs on a consistent schedule, undergoing none of the stresses usually associated with his office.

This deal against one of the American teams began France's surge towards victory on the final day:

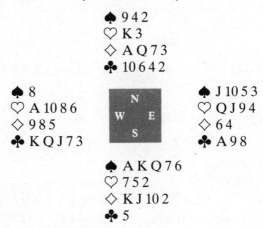

```
                    ♠ 9 4 2
                    ♡ K 3
                    ◇ A Q 7 3
                    ♣ 10 6 4 2
    ♠ 8                            ♠ J 10 5 3
    ♡ A 10 8 6                     ♡ Q J 9 4
    ◇ 9 8 5                        ◇ 6 4
    ♣ K Q J 7 3                    ♣ A 9 8
                    ♠ A K Q 7 6
                    ♡ 7 5 2
                    ◇ K J 10 2
                    ♣ 5
```

At game all the bidding went:

South Delmouly	West Mitchell	North Bourchtoff	East Rubin
—	No	No	No
1♠	Dble	Redble	2♡
No	No	2♠	No
3◇	3♡	4◇	No
4♠	No	No	No

[84]

The defence began with two rounds of clubs. South ruffed, led a heart to the king, then a second heart, won by East, who continued with a third club. South had to ruff again, and the position was now:

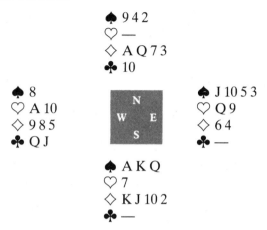

```
                    ♠ 9 4 2
                    ♡ —
                    ◇ A Q 7 3
                    ♣ 10
    ♠ 8                           ♠ J 10 5 3
    ♡ A 10          N             ♡ Q 9
    ◇ 9 8 5      W     E          ◇ 6 4
    ♣ Q J          S              ♣ —
                    ♠ A K Q
                    ♡ 7
                    ◇ K J 10 2
                    ♣ —
```

Delmouly drew just one round of trumps, then ruffed this heart loser and played on diamonds. East ruffed the third round but was now helpless: if he led a heart, dummy would ruff while South disposed of his fourth diamond.

If declarer had drawn a second round of trumps in the diagram position he would have been defeated, East making the last two tricks with a trump and a heart.

Point to remember: When a player who has passed originally later makes a take-out double and raises his partner's response, you can be sure that he has 'shape', including a singleton or void of the suit he doubled.

Passing of a Star

The American player, Lew Mathe, who died in 1986, attracted much interest when he played in the 1954 world championship match in Monte Carlo. He was the main architect of victory against a European team that included French, Swiss and Austrian players. I wrote in *Le Figaro*, 'He smokes giant-sized cigars, chewing gum at the same time. On top of this, he has an extraordinary collection of many-hued ties and shirts . . .'

Mathe's best performance was in the 1962 world championship, when the Americans finished second to the Italians, then at the top of their form. His play on the following deal, it was said, raised the roof of the Barbizon Hotel in New York.

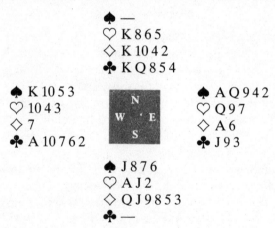

```
              ♠ —
              ♡ K 8 6 5
              ◇ K 10 4 2
              ♣ K Q 8 5 4
♠ K 10 5 3              ♠ A Q 9 4 2
♡ 10 4 3               ♡ Q 9 7
◇ 7                    ◇ A 6
♣ A 10 7 6 2           ♣ J 9 3
              ♠ J 8 7 6
              ♡ A J 2
              ◇ Q J 9 8 5 3
              ♣ —
```

At game all the bidding went:

South	West	North	East
Mathe	Belladonna	Nail	Avarelli
—	No	No	1♠
2◇	4♠	6◇	No
No	Dble	No	No
No			

West led the 3 of spades and dummy ruffed. The king of clubs was led from the table, and when East played low Mathe ruffed. He continued with spade and club ruffs to reach the following position:

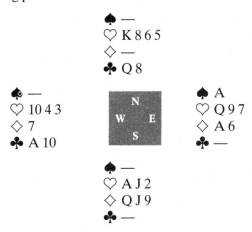

Now he yielded just one trick to the ace of trumps.

The play was not so simple, as may be judged from the fact that at the other table Chiaradia went one down in *five* diamonds. He ruffed the spade lead, then let the king of clubs run to West's ace. The defence now played two rounds of trumps. South had lost two tricks and could still have succeeded with a heart finesse. Instead he played for a squeeze against West in hearts and clubs, so losing the last trick to ♡Q.

Point to remember: When a king from K Q is led from dummy early in the play, and the next defender does not cover, it is fair to suppose that the ace is held by his partner.

T.R. adds: The Italians seem not to have been at their best on this deal. West, surely, should have led a trump against six diamonds, a contract that would only be made on crossruff lines. And Chiaradia, after the spade lead, should have crossruffed instead of running the king of clubs. Just two tricks in hearts and nine in trumps would win the money.

Noxious Weed

Back in 1967 I wrote: 'For several years bidding systems have sprouted like noxious weeds. It seems that in every bridge player there is a lurking inventor. Even though the results are not always happy, the virus is particularly active among certain champions. It is rare, in international play, to find two pairs who play the same system . . .' This is true of everyone today except the French, who, happily, almost all play the same style.

In the Tournament of Champions at Deauville in 1967 each of the eight pairs played a different system. Georges Théron played cleverly on this deal after an opponent had made a semi-psychic bid of a familiar type.

```
            ♠ K 10 8 6 5
            ♡ Q 9 6
            ♦ 7 3
            ♣ J 7 4

♦ K led

            ♠ 7
            ♡ A K 10 7 5 3
            ♦ 9 6 2
            ♣ A K 8
```

With North–South vulnerable the bidding went:

South	West	North	East
Théron	Reese	Desrousseaux	Flint
1♡	1NT	2♡	No
3♦	Dble	4♡	No
No	No		

West led the king of diamonds and followed with a diamond to his partner's ace. East returned a low trump. How do you think Théron played now?

It was fairly clear that West's 1NT overcall was based on a long diamond suit. In this case the majority of the outstanding strength would be held by East. If East held the ace of spades and the queen of clubs, there would be a chance for a throw-in.

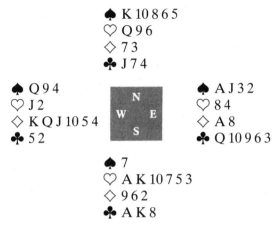

♠ K 10 8 6 5
♡ Q 9 6
♢ 7 3
♣ J 7 4

♠ Q 9 4
♡ J 2
♢ K Q J 10 5 4
♣ 5 2

♠ A J 3 2
♡ 8 4
♢ A 8
♣ Q 10 9 6 3

♠ 7
♡ A K 10 7 5 3
♢ 9 6 2
♣ A K 8

After king and ace of diamonds South won the heart return in dummy, crossed to the king of clubs, and ruffed his third diamond. Then he played off all his trumps. East, down to the ace of spades and Q 10 of clubs, was thrown in and forced to concede the last two tricks.

When the play ended, Reese reproached* his partner for not overtaking the king of diamonds at trick one and returning the suit. Then a third diamond might tempt declarer to ruff with the queen and later lose a trump trick to West's jack.

Point to remember: When a player overcalls with a 'comic' notrump he will hold little or no strength outside his long suit. Note, incidentally, that Flint judged the situation well, passing over two North's hearts.

---

* Not 'reproached', surely; just sort of mentioned, perhaps.—T.R.

In a Class of Her Own

Among all the champions who have dominated women's bridge, Rixi Markus is in a class of her own, especially in the play of the cards. Her partnership with Fritzi Gordon, in the years from 1960 to 1970, was in the same class as the strongest of men. It is notable, too, that Rixi has achieved so many fine performances with a wide variety of partners. Here is an example of a slam contract that she described to me in one of her letters. 'I am sending you', she wrote, 'with my best wishes for 1969, a slam on which all the other players failed during our recent selection trials'.

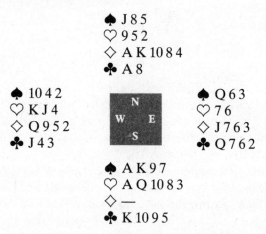

```
                    ♠ J 8 5
                    ♡ 9 5 2
                    ◇ A K 10 8 4
                    ♣ A 8
    ♠ 10 4 2                        ♠ Q 6 3
    ♡ K J 4          N              ♡ 7 6
    ◇ Q 9 5 2      W   E            ◇ J 7 6 3
    ♣ J 4 3          S              ♣ Q 7 6 2
                    ♠ A K 9 7
                    ♡ A Q 10 8 3
                    ◇ —
                    ♣ K 10 9 5
```

South played in six hearts and West led the 2 of diamonds. Most players, no doubt, took at least one finesse in trumps and reckoned they had been unlucky.

Rixi had a different approach. She ruffed the diamond lead and her first move was to cash the ace and king of spades. Then she crossed to the ace of clubs, discarded two spades on the top diamonds, and ruffed the fourth round of diamonds successfully. After king of clubs and a club ruff the position was:

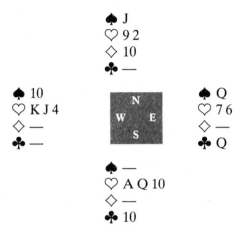

♠ J
♡ 9 2
♢ 10
♣ —

♠ 10   ♠ Q
♡ K J 4   ♡ 7 6
♢ —   ♢ —
♣ —   ♣ Q

♠ —
♡ A Q 10
♢ —
♣ 10

Now Rixi ruffed the jack of spades with the 10 of hearts and led the 10 of clubs from hand. As you see, it would not help West to ruff with the jack of hearts; so long as East held the fourth club the contract would be safe.

You may think at first that the natural play would be to take two finesses in trumps. That is not right, because declarer's general plan is to discard two spades on the A K of diamonds and to take two club ruffs in dummy.

Point to note: On certain hands the best plan is to cash winners and crossruff—especially when the opening lead (here the 2 of diamonds) suggests that there will be no early overruff.

Miracle Slam

Sometimes there's no justice in bridge, as is shown by the almost impossible slam that was made on this deal:

```
            ♠ 9 7 6 4
            ♡ 8 4
            ◇ 5 4
            ♣ A Q 10 3 2
♣ 6 led
            ♠ A 10
            ♡ K Q J 2
            ◇ A Q J 7 6
            ♣ K 5
```

With no-one vulnerable, at rubber bridge, the bidding went:

South	West	North	East
Le Dentu	Riem	X . . .	Henry
2◇	No	3♣	No
3♡	No	4◇	No
4NT	No	5◇	No
6◇	No	No	No

My partner had insisted on natural bidding apart from two clubs and Blackwood. My opening two diamonds was an attempt to conform, but I admit it wasn't a good choice.

Having said that, I have to place some of the blame on my partner. It was wrong to respond three clubs on such moderate values; the first response should be 2NT. Still worse was the preference to four diamonds on the second round.

Well, there you are—there I was—in six diamonds, West leading a low club. Do you see *any* chance of making this contract without some help from the defence? It is quite a testing problem.

To begin with, you will need to make all five diamonds, which means that you must find East with K x x. The clubs have to be 3-3, so that you can discard your spade loser. To gain the entries for two trump leads, you will need the 10 of clubs to hold the first trick. Finally, since you will have no opportunity to lead hearts from the table, you must hope to find a singleton ace somewhere. And so it all was, the full hand being:

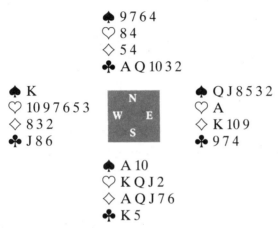

- ♠ 9 7 6 4
- ♡ 8 4
- ♢ 5 4
- ♣ A Q 10 3 2

- ♠ K
- ♡ 10 9 7 6 5 3
- ♢ 8 3 2
- ♣ J 8 6

- ♠ Q J 8 5 3 2
- ♡ A
- ♢ K 10 9
- ♣ 9 7 4

- ♠ A 10
- ♡ K Q J 2
- ♢ A Q J 7 6
- ♣ K 5

You see the sequence of play? Club 10, diamond finesse, overtake club king, discard on club queen, diamond finesse, ace of diamonds. Now all you need, if you believe in fairies, is to lead a low heart and find someone with the singleton ace.

Considered independently, the chances were something like this: West with three clubs to the jack, about one chance in six; same for finding East with three diamonds to the king; ace of hearts single, about one chance in 100. Altogether, something in the region of 3600 to 1.

Point to remember: There's not much to say except . . . never give up! The opponents may make some terrible mistake or there may be a miracle in the distribution.

Sensation in London

One evening in 1950, at the club Albarran, a young man in uniform asked if he could join our table.

'We're playing fairly high', we said, naming the stake.

'That's all right'.

At the end of the session I asked him his name.

'Henri Svarc.'

'You'll be champion of France by next year'.

And so he was!

Svarc is the most gifted of all our great players. In 1978, playing in the *Sunday Times* tournament, he made a sensational grand slam after Boulenger had made a timid opening on a big hand. These were the North–South cards:

    ♠ K Q 7 3
    ♡ —
    ♢ A K J 10 8 6
    ♣ A Q J

♡ K led

    ♠ A 8 4 2
    ♡ 10 5 4
    ♢ Q 2
    ♣ 9 8 4 3

This was the bidding at game all:

South	West	North	East
Svarc	Brock	Boulenger	Pencharz
—	—	—	No
No	No	1♢	No
1♠	No	3♣	No
3♢	No	3♠	No
4♠	No	5♡	No
5♠	No	6♡	No
7♠	No	No	No

West led the king of hearts. How do you imagine that South made the grand slam *even though the king of clubs was held by East?* You won't find it easy to judge even with a view of all the cards.

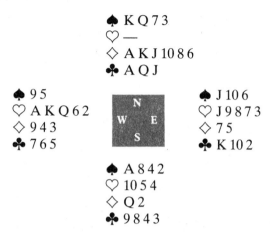

                    ♠ K Q 7 3
                    ♡ —
                    ◇ A K J 10 8 6
                    ♣ A Q J

    ♠ 9 5   ♠ J 10 6
    ♡ A K Q 6 2   ♡ J 9 8 7 3
    ◇ 9 4 3   ◇ 7 5
    ♣ 7 6 5   ♣ K 10 2

                    ♠ A 8 4 2
                    ♡ 10 5 4
                    ◇ Q 2
                    ♣ 9 8 4 3

Henri ruffed the heart lead in dummy, drew two rounds of trumps with the K Q of spades, and crossed to the queen of diamonds.

He had decided already that the club finesse was likely to be wrong. (West had passed in third position although he was marked with a good suit of hearts.) Instead of drawing the outstanding trump, Svarc played two more rounds of diamonds. East ruffed (no difference if he waits), and South overruffed. Then he crossed to the ace of clubs, discarded three clubs on the diamonds, took the ruffing finesse in clubs, and ruffed a heart to make the last trick with the jack of clubs.

Point to note: The declarer had first to realise that the club finesse was probably wrong, and second, that it might be possible to discard three clubs on the long diamonds and then take the backward finesse.

A Psychological Safety Play

It is possible, on occasions, to develop a suit in a way that may cause an opponent to play low when he should be taking his winner. He may then be liable to a throw-in.

```
                    ♠ A K 8
                    ♡ K J 8 3
                    ◇ Q 10 4
                    ♣ 9 7 5
     ♠ Q J 10 7 3      N        ♠ 9 6 2
     ♡ 9 2          W     E      ♡ Q 10 7 5
     ◇ 9 8 5 2                   ◇ J 7 6
     ♣ 10 3            S         ♣ A 4 2
                    ♠ 5 4
                    ♡ A 6 4
                    ◇ A K 3
                    ♣ K Q J 8 6
```

North–South had a part score of 60, which did not make the bidding any easier. It went like this:

South	West	North	East
Le Dentu	Charles	Sutter	Lamielle
1NT	No	2NT	No
3♣	No	3♡	No
4♣	No	5♣	No
5◇	No	6♣	all pass

From a part score of 60 it is always sensible to extend the range of a 1NT opening from something like 12 points (non-vulnerable) to 21. It is a dangerous bid to overcall and you avoid the hazard of opening 2NT on 20 to 21 points and finding that you can make only seven tricks.

On the present hand we managed the bidding well, I think—at least, my partner did. His 2NT gave me a chance to express a big hand, and his raise to five clubs was well judged.

Henri Charles led the queen of spades against six clubs, and I won in dummy. It looked as though the contract would depend on the heart finesse. However, I saw that it might be possible to play the trumps in a slightly deceptive way. I led a club to the king at trick two and could then have led the queen of clubs from hand (still picking up East's A 10 x x, if necessary). Instead, I crossed to the queen of diamonds and led another low club from the table. Now East, with his mind on the club situation, played low again, because it was quite possible that I held K Q 10 x x and would need to take a view on this trick.

When the queen of clubs held I played a spade to the king and ruffed the third round, then drew two more rounds of diamonds. You see the position now?

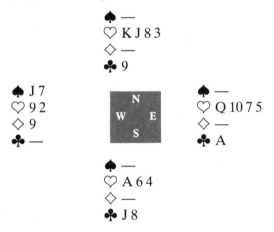

A club from hand left East on play.

Point to remember: When you have 60 on score, open 1NT on balanced hands in the range of 12 to 21, or 14 to 21 if you are vulnerable. With 13 points or more it will always be safe for partner to raise to 2NT.

[97]

'Don't you sometimes run short of material?' bridge writers are often asked. Not really; apart from deals played in important matches, in every session of rubber bridge there is a hand worth writing about. Consider this deal from a friendly game at Cannes:

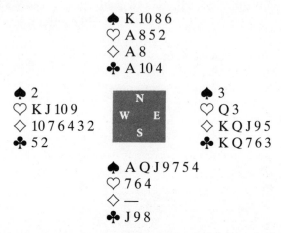

```
                    ♠ K 10 8 6
                    ♡ A 8 5 2
                    ◇ A 8
                    ♣ A 10 4
      ♠ 2                              ♠ 3
      ♡ K J 10 9                       ♡ Q 3
      ◇ 10 7 6 4 3 2                   ◇ K Q J 9 5
      ♣ 5 2                            ♣ K Q 7 6 3
                    ♠ A Q J 9 7 5 4
                    ♡ 7 6 4
                    ◇ —
                    ♣ J 9 8
```

Neither side was vulnerable, but North–South had a part score of 40. This accounts for the bidding, which was as follows:

South	West	North	East
Le Dentu	Dehaussy	Hart	Chazal
—	—	1♣	1◇
1♠	2◇	2♠	3◇
3♠	4◇	4♠	No
No	5◇	Dble	No
5♠	No	No	No

West led a low diamond and I noted that I could discard a heart on the ace of diamonds and make the contract if the hearts were breaking 3-3 or if just one of the club honours were held by West. Unfortunately for my team, West won an early trick in hearts and switched to a club. I found myself losing one heart and two clubs, which was rather poor if only because we could have taken 300 from five diamonds doubled.

I like to think that if I had been playing in a tournament I would have made this contract. It is better to play low from dummy on the diamond lead and discard a heart from my own hand. Another heart is discarded on the ace of diamonds, and after testing the hearts I arrive at this position:

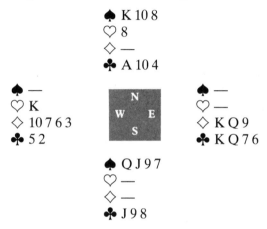

```
              ♠ K 10 8
              ♡ 8
              ♢ —
              ♣ A 10 4
♠ —                              ♠ —
♡ K                              ♡ —
♢ 10 7 6 3                       ♢ K Q 9
♣ 5 2                            ♣ K Q 7 6
              ♠ Q J 9 7
              ♡ —
              ♢ —
              ♣ J 9 8
```

Very simple now to run the 8 of clubs and make the contract against any return.

Point to remember: Looking at the hand again, I see that winning the first trick with the ace of diamonds should not have been fatal. I can ruff a diamond, draw a round of trumps, then play ace and another heart. If West wins and exits with a club, East will be on play after taking the queen. Not my day!

The Invisible Trick

Players who have the gambling instinct like to play goulashes at rubber bridge. The cards are sorted and are dealt in groups of 5-5-3 instead of the sedate one at a time. Freakish hands are common and bidding technique is quite different from the normal game. This was one such deal:

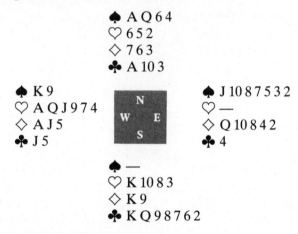

```
              ♠ A Q 6 4
              ♡ 6 5 2
              ◇ 7 6 3
              ♣ A 10 3
♠ K 9                          ♠ J 10 8 7 5 3 2
♡ A Q J 9 7 4       N          ♡ —
◇ A J 5          W     E       ◇ Q 10 8 4 2
♣ J 5               S          ♣ 4
              ♠ —
              ♡ K 10 8 3
              ◇ K 9
              ♣ K Q 9 8 7 6 2
```

At game all the bidding went:

South	West	North	East
Tintner	*Palau*	*Milchten*	*Sarfati*
3♣	3♡	5♣	No
No	No		

West led the 9 of spades against five clubs. It may seem a strange choice, but he had no good alternative and the ace of spades was likely to be on his left. How do you suppose that Léon Tintner made his contract against best defence?

To begin with, obviously, he had to try the queen of spades, which held the trick. He followed with the ace of spades, discarding *diamonds* on these two tricks. Then he ruffed a diamond and made another critical play, finessing the 10 of clubs. Using the two trump entries, he ruffed the remaining diamonds, to reach the following position:

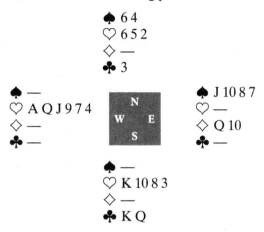

```
                      ♠ 6 4
                      ♡ 6 5 2
                      ◇ —
                      ♣ 3

        ♠ —                          ♠ J 10 8 7
        ♡ A Q J 9 7 4    N           ♡ —
        ◇ —           W     E        ◇ Q 10
        ♣ —              S           ♣ —

                      ♠ —
                      ♡ K 10 8 3
                      ◇ —
                      ♣ K Q
```

Now Léon advanced the 10 of hearts, confident that West (who had overcalled in hearts at the three level) would have to win the trick. West could only return the suit and there was still a trump in dummy for the fourth round.

Point to remember: The immediate finesse of the 10 of clubs was necessary because, in the end-game, the declarer would need a trump in each hand. Otherwise West, after winning with ♡J, would return a low heart and make two more tricks.

A Protest at Djerba

A contract of six spades does not, at first sight, seem attractive on this deal from the 1980 Festival of Djerba. As you see, the trumps were 5-0 and there was an ace missing.

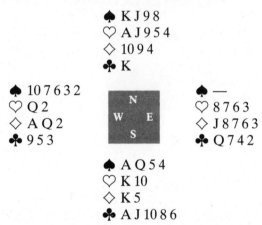

♠ K J 9 8
♥ A J 9 5 4
♦ 10 9 4
♣ K

♠ 10 7 6 3 2
♥ Q 2
♦ A Q 2
♣ 9 5 3

♠ —
♥ 8 7 6 3
♦ J 8 7 6 3
♣ Q 7 4 2

♠ A Q 5 4
♥ K 10
♦ K 5
♣ A J 10 8 6

At least two French internationals bid and made the slam in spades. This was the bidding at one table:

South	West	North	East
Abecassis	Desrousseaux	Chemla	Sabouret
—	No	1♥	No
2♣	No	2♥	No
2♠	No	3♠	No
4♦	No	5♣	No
6♠	No	No	No

Hoping to make a trump trick, Ursula Desrousseaux laid down the ace of diamonds and followed with the 2 of spades. When the trump situation was revealed, the declarer cashed two hearts, king of diamonds, and two clubs. A diamond ruff and a club ruff brought him to eight tricks, and it wasn't difficult to make the last four tricks with a high crossruff.

Nothing very exciting or strange in this, you may think, but two other happenings on this deal deserve to be recorded.

At one table the contract was 6NT and the West player, having heard the opponents bid spades, hearts and clubs, made the remarkable lead of the 2 of diamonds. Such leads are sometimes 'the only way to beat the contract', but not on this occasion. The king of diamonds was the twelfth trick.

At another table North–South reached the natural contract of six spades, whereupon West doubled. Taken by surprise, North pondered for a few moments before passing. At once West called 'Director!' When the official arrived, West outlined his case:

'I doubled six spades and this man (politely indicating his left-hand opponent) hesitated before passing. He may have been thinking of transferring to 6NT. In any case, I claim that South must pass.'

While the Director searched for his rule book, the South player, a Belgian named Rosenberg, said he was quite happy to pass. So the hand was played in six spades doubled and when this was made (after the same lead of the ace of diamonds) the obstreperous West was rewarded with what in France is called a *zero intégral*.

Point to remember: West would have been wiser to let South play in 6NT, if he wanted to, and reserve his rights. As it happens, there are only eleven tricks in notrumps.

The Magician of Juan

The great English player, John Collings, who lived in the south of France for many years, has a brilliant record in the Individual at Juan-les-Pins. It requires a special technique to do well in this three-session event where you have a different partner and opponents every couple of boards.

```
                    ♠ 10 3 2
                    ♡ A Q 10 2
                    ◇ A 6 2
                    ♣ K 8 7
    ♠ 4                            ♠ 7 6 5
    ♡ K 9 3          N             ♡ J 8 6 4
    ◇ K Q 10 8 4 3  W   E          ◇ J 9
    ♣ 10 5 4          S            ♣ Q J 9 2
                    ♠ A K Q J 9 8
                    ♡ 7 5
                    ◇ 7 5
                    ♣ A 6 3
```

With North–South vulnerable, and Collings South, the bidding went:

South	West	North	East
—	4◇ (1)	No	4♠ (2)
Dble	No	No	5◇
5♠	No	6♡ (3)	No
6♠	No	No	No

(1) When John appears on the scene most of his opponents will try . . .

(2) . . . anything.

(3) What am I supposed to do, she wonders.

West began with the king of diamonds. Remembering that East had supported the pre-emptive opening, Collings played low, to improve the timing for a possible squeeze. West led another diamond, won by the ace.

In a minute at most the hand was over. South drew trumps, finessed the queen of hearts, and ruffed the third round. Another round of trumps brought about this position:

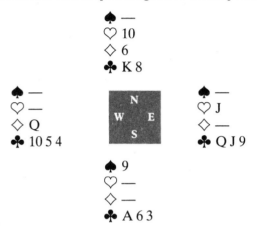

On the last trump, a club from West, a diamond from North, and East was squeezed.

Point to remember: When planning a squeeze, it is usually necessary to lose a trick early on, to bring about the situation where you can make all the remaining tricks but one. It was difficult to foresee, but a club from West at trick two is the best defence.

The Finesse with Nine

Most players have heard of the saying 'eight ever, nine never', meaning that with eight cards it is right to finesse for a queen, but with nine to play for the drop. It is right, however, to take note of the distribution of the nine cards between the declarer and the dummy. If the division is 7-2 (such as K x and A J 10 x x x x) the whole hand is likely to be unbalanced and it is right to finesse. With 6-3 the decision is close; with 5-4 it is better to play for the drop.*

Of course, there may be special considerations, arising from the opponents' bidding—or even their silence.

```
                    ♠ 7
                    ♡ K J 10 8
                    ♢ K Q 9 8 4
                    ♣ Q 6 2

     ♢ 3 led

                    ♠ A
                    ♡ A 9 7 6 2
                    ♢ A J 6 2
                    ♣ A 5 3
```

South	West	North	East
Morin	Rochecouste	Le Dentu	Poumaillou
—	—	1♢	No
2♡	No	3♡	No
3♠	No	4♡	No
4NT	No	5♣	No
5NT	No	6♡	all pass

*Mathematicians wouldn't agree with this analysis. According to them, the division between North and South cannot affect the division between East and West.—T.R.

Having opened the bidding on a minimum hand I thought it right to hold back afterwards. West led the 3 of diamonds, a possible singleton. Do you think that South should play for the trumps to be 2-2 or 3-1?

Jean Morin looked at it this way:

1. If the 3 of diamonds was a singleton, West would be likely to hold three trumps.

2. Whether or not the lead was a singleton, West might have chosen it to frighten the declarer into drawing the top trumps. Players with Q x x in the trump suit sometimes do that.

My partner's theory turned out to be right, for the full hand was:

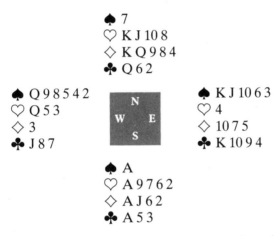

♠ 7
♡ K J 10 8
◇ K Q 9 8 4
♣ Q 6 2

♠ Q 9 8 5 4 2
♡ Q 5 3
◇ 3
♣ J 8 7

♠ K J 10 6 3
♡ 4
◇ 10 7 5
♣ K 10 9 4

♠ A
♡ A 9 7 6 2
◇ A J 6 2
♣ A 5 3

South won the diamond lead, cashed ace of spades, then played ace of hearts and successfully finessed the jack.

Point to remember: When you are missing four to the queen the theoretical advantage of playing for a 2-2 break is quite small. It is right, therefore, to take note of any special indications.

Clash of the Titans

The Tournament of Champions at Deauville is always a great occasion, and never more so than when Paul Chemla and Benito Garozzo are in opposition. Observe this dramatic deal from the 1985 event.

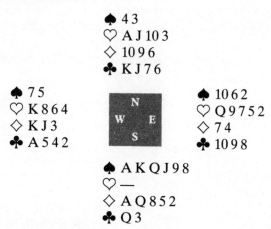

                    ♠ 4 3
                    ♡ A J 10 3
                    ◇ 10 9 6
                    ♣ K J 7 6

    ♠ 7 5   ♠ 10 6 2
    ♡ K 8 6 4   ♡ Q 9 7 5 2
    ◇ K J 3   ◇ 7 4
    ♣ A 5 4 2   ♣ 10 9 8

                    ♠ A K Q J 9 8
                    ♡ —
                    ◇ A Q 8 5 2
                    ♣ Q 3

At game all the bidding went:

South	West	North	East
Chemla	Garozzo	Perron	Ferraro
2♣	No	2♡	No
2♠	No	3♣	No
3◇	No	4NT	No
5♠	No	6♠	all pass

North's two hearts was ace-showing, so over three diamonds on the third round he might simply have bid three hearts instead of the non-conventional 4NT.

West began with a trump against six spades. Prospects do not look at all good, do they? Even if South succeeds in sneaking a club trick and discarding his second club on the ace of hearts he will still lose two diamonds, apparently.

South drew trumps, then led the 3 of clubs. Garozzo went in with the ace and led a heart. Dummy's 10 was headed by the queen and ruffed by the declarer. Chemla led all his remaining trumps, then overtook the queen of clubs. After the next club the position was:

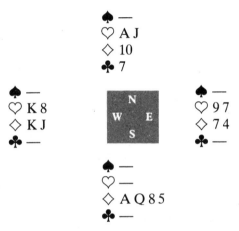

On the last club Garozzo bared his king of diamonds, but Chemla knew what was happening: he cashed the ace of hearts and then, to a storm of applause, the ace of diamonds.

Point to remember: Maybe West should have reflected that with Q 10 9 8 of clubs his partner would have dropped the 10 under the ace. If he places East instead with 10 9 8, then a club back is the best defence.

Masterly Deception

The cleverest trick of 1986 took place in the Patton (teams-of-four) at Deauville. It was as though an acrobat made a perfect landing after his safety net had broken.

                     ♠ A Q 10 4
                     ♡ K J 10 9
                     ◇ K J 10 9 6
                     ♣ —

♣ J led

                     ♠ J
                     ♡ Q 3
                     ◇ Q 8 7 5 4 3
                     ♣ A Q 6 4

South opened very light and soon had cause to regret it:

South	West	North	East
Sussel	X . . .	De Lesleuc	Y . . .
1◇	No	1♡	1♠
No	2♠	6◇	No
No	No		

West led the jack of clubs. How could South escape the loss of two aces?

Patrick Sussel ruffed the first trick and led a low spade from dummy at trick two!

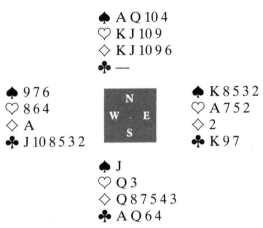

```
              ♠ A Q 10 4
              ♡ K J 10 9
              ◇ K J 10 9 6
              ♣ —
♠ 9 7 6                      ♠ K 8 5 3 2
♡ 8 6 4                      ♡ A 7 5 2
◇ A                          ◇ 2
♣ J 10 8 5 3 2               ♣ K 9 7
              ♠ J
              ♡ Q 3
              ◇ Q 8 7 5 4 3
              ♣ A Q 6 4
```

East assumed, naturally enough, that South was void in spades and played low. Now the declarer returned to dummy with a club ruff and led ace, followed by queen of spades, which East covered. Back to dummy with another club ruff, and the second heart went away on the 10 of spades, while West had to ruff with the ace of trumps—the only trick for his side.

Point to remember: When dummy holds a side suit headed by the A Q, and the declarer holds a singleton jack, with the king known to be off-side, a low card from dummy may win a surprise trick.

T.R. adds: This was clever play, widely admired at the time. There must be other possibilities of the same kind. For example, with A K J x x in dummy, singleton 10 in hand, a low card from dummy might well deceive a defender who held such as Q 9 x x.

Our Man in Caracas

This fine deal was like a praying mantis that devoured almost all the declarers in the eliminating round of the Central American Championship, played at Caracas in 1987. Six spades was the contract at several tables, but it was made only once.

The exception was Mohan Seepersad of Trinidad, who cleverly took note of West's heart overcall.

```
              ♠ 7 2
              ♡ 4 3
              ◇ A 10 4 2
              ♣ Q J 10 9 8

   ♡ K led

              ♠ A K Q 10 9 6
              ♡ A 7 6 5 2
              ◇ —
              ♣ A K
```

The bidding was usually on these lines:

South	West	North	East
2♣	2♡	3◇	No
3♠	No	4♣	No
4♡	No	4♠	No
6♠	No	No	No

North's three diamonds in this sequence is ace-showing. West leads the king of hearts. How should South organise the play?

[112]

The usual line was to cash a couple of clubs and return a low heart. This could not possibly win, because East would be discarding a club on the second heart. Even if East could not overruff dummy's 7 of spades on the third round of hearts, South would not obtain sufficient discards.

The Trinidadian followed a simple enough line, which you would hardly miss, looking at the full deal:

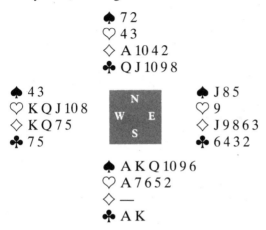

```
                ♠ 7 2
                ♡ 4 3
                ◇ A 10 4 2
                ♣ Q J 10 9 8
♠ 4 3                         ♠ J 8 5
♡ K Q J 10 8                  ♡ 9
◇ K Q 7 5                     ◇ J 9 8 6 3
♣ 7 5                         ♣ 6 4 3 2
                ♠ A K Q 10 9 6
                ♡ A 7 6 5 2
                ◇ —
                ♣ A K
```

After winning the first trick with the ace of hearts, South cashed two spades, ace and king of clubs, then exited with the 6 of spades. Curtains!

Meanwhile, players who returned a heart at trick two tended to finish one down in *four* spades, losing all four low hearts.

Point to remember: As I dare say you have noted, East also had an opportunity for fine play—by dropping the 8 and jack of spades under the ace and king!

PART IV

Great Catastrophes

No-one can escape the occasional catastrophe. They cause shivers to the players, but the rest of the world will find them amusing. The ones I describe here are among the most astonishing, but they are also, in their way, instructive.

If you think that on each occasion you would yourself have escaped misfortune—well, bravo for your confidence.

Sensational Support

The setting was perfect: a packed audience at the Casino Municipal in Cannes watching the annual encounter between the best players of France and Italy. On board 19 the bidding on bridgerama was normal; in the closed room one bid shook all the seismographs.

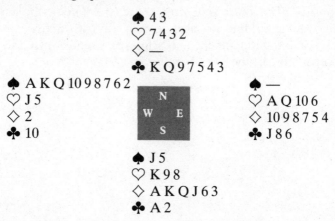

♠ 4 3
♡ 7 4 3 2
◇ —
♣ K Q 9 7 5 4 3

♠ A K Q 10 9 8 7 6 2
♡ J 5
◇ 2
♣ 10

♠ —
♡ A Q 10 6
◇ 10 9 8 7 5 4
♣ J 8 6

♠ J 5
♡ K 9 8
◇ A K Q J 6 3
♣ A 2

At game to East–West the bidding on Rama was as follows:

South Sbarigia	West Mari	North Rosati	East Perron
—	—	No	No
1◇	4♣	No	No
5◇	No	No	Dble
No	No	No	

Note West's prudent pass over five diamonds.

West led two top spades, on which East discarded two clubs. South lost in all two spades, two hearts, and two trumps. 700 to East–West looked pretty good to the home supporters, but a shock was in store. In the closed room the bidding went:

South	West	North	East
Stoppa	Avarelli	X . . .	Pabis Ticci
—	—	3♣	No
3◇	4♠	No	No
5◇	5♠	No	No
6♣	No	No	Dble
No	No	6◇!	Dble
No	No	No	

When the bid of six diamonds was announced from the closed room, I said on the commentator's microphone that there must have been an error in transmission. Not so! Six diamonds was five down, 900 to Italy.

You may not have noticed the most extraordinary thing about this deal. Because East cannot lead a spade, North cannot be defeated in six clubs.

Ace and another heart is the best that East can do. North wins in dummy, leads a club to the king, and a club back to the ace. Now a miserable East can only follow suit while the declarer takes four discards on the top diamonds. Then a heart is ruffed and the last trump is drawn.

None of which adds to the charm of North's six diamond call!

A Small Misunderstanding

Playing rubber bridge at the Cannes club (where the standard of play is extremely variable), you pick up this hand, not vulnerable:

♠ 10 9 4
♡ 10 9 8 7 6 4 3
♢ 5
♣ 6 5

Your partner passes—bad news. East, on your right, opens two clubs—worse news.

You are going to lose a small slam at least, so you must try some counteraction. Not wanting to go too far over the top at rubber bridge, I decided that a fairly cautious three hearts would be as good as anything.

And now the question: what game contract would you be happy for the opponents to reach? Game in hearts, to be sure, and your prayers are answered when the bidding goes:

South	West	North	East
—	—	No	2♣
3♡	4♡	No	No
No			

What has happened? This was the full hand:

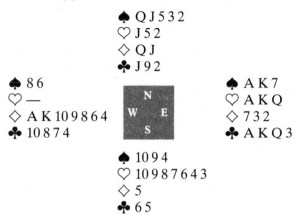

```
                    ♠ Q J 5 3 2
                    ♡ J 5 2
                    ◇ Q J
                    ♣ J 9 2
   ♠ 8 6                              ♠ A K 7
   ♡ —                               ♡ A K Q
   ◇ A K 10 9 8 6 4                  ◇ 7 3 2
   ♣ 10 8 7 4                        ♣ A K Q 3
                    ♠ 10 9 4
                    ♡ 10 9 8 7 6 4 3
                    ◇ 5
                    ♣ 6 5
```

Defending against four hearts, I made four trumps and a spade.

Whose fault was it? West could have bid a straightforward five diamonds. East evidently thought that my three hearts was a psychic based on long diamonds (these horrid professionals!) What he thought his partner was likely to hold is another question.

T.R. adds: Although the outcome was different, this episode reminded me of the famous occasion in the European Championship at Ostend in 1965. East opened two clubs and John Collings, South, held a yarborough with a singleton spade. His selected overcall? Four spades!

His partner, Jonathan Cansino, held some support for spades, but kept silent until the opponents bid to a grand slam in another suit. Jonathan then came in with seven spades, which went for something over 2000, made worse by the fact that their team-mates had bid only a small slam.

The British non-playing captain, Reg Corwen, didn't think it funny and declared that Collings would never play another board for Britain under his captaincy.

The Hidden Sacrifice

To fail to cash a winner and lose touch with it is something that normally happens only to beginners. To do this deliberately in a grand slam contract would make Machiavelli himself jealous. The success of this stratagem was a calamity for the British team and contributed to France's victory in the 1985 Common Market championship.

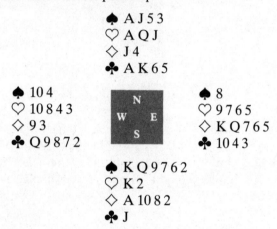

```
                    ♠ A J 5 3
                    ♡ A Q J
                    ◇ J 4
                    ♣ A K 6 5
  ♠ 10 4                             ♠ 8
  ♡ 10 8 4 3          N             ♡ 9 7 6 5
  ◇ 9 3           W       E         ◇ K Q 7 6 5
  ♣ Q 9 8 7 2         S             ♣ 10 4 3
                    ♠ K Q 9 7 6 2
                    ♡ K 2
                    ◇ A 10 8 2
                    ♣ J
```

At love all the bidding went:

| South | West | North | East |
Desrousseaux	Forrester	Crozet	Lodge
—	No	1♣	1◇
1♠	No	4♠	No
4NT	No	5♣	No
7♠	No	No	No

This was standard bidding. North's raise to four spades implied a strong balanced hand, because with a singleton he would have made some kind of splinter bid. The response of five clubs showed 0 or 3 aces. South might have wondered how he was going to avoid a diamond loser, it is true.

And he must still have wondered when the dummy went down, revealing some duplication of values in hearts and clubs. Do you see any way to escape the diamond loser?

West's lead of the 9 of diamonds was covered by the queen and ace. South tried the jack of clubs at trick two, perhaps intending to run it, but West covered. After drawing trumps South discarded the 10 of diamonds on the third heart and played for this ending:

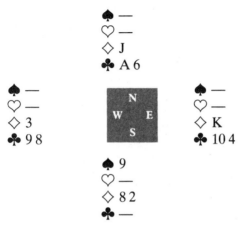

South led the 9 of spades and threw the jack of diamonds from dummy. East fell into the trap and discarded his king of diamonds. The defence was imperfect*, no doubt, but it was still a brilliant pseudo-squeeze.

At the other table the British North–South, Smolski and Stanley, had done well—thought they had done well—to stop in six spades.

* Yes; for one thing, if South had held J 9 x of clubs, he would hardly have begun with the jack.—T.R.

The Curse of the Aces

Every year in the world championships there are misunderstandings to remind us that the human brain has its limits. The most famous of all was the grand slam in hearts bid by Trézel against the Brazilians with four aces missing. (The response of five clubs to 4NT signified 0 or 4 aces, and somebody drew the wrong conclusion!)

Earlier in the same year the so-called Dallas Aces, who for several months had been training for eight hours a day, reached a grand slam in clubs after exchanging fourteen bids. Unlucky, Jaïs led the ace of diamonds and nobody could ruff.

Two years later, in the Bermuda Bowl at Guaruja (Brazil), there was a deal about which the *Bridge World* wrote: 'You would have to see this deal no. 90 to believe it. You would think it was fiction, but it really happened.'

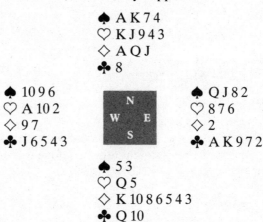

```
              ♠ A K 7 4
              ♡ K J 9 4 3
              ◇ A Q J
              ♣ 8
♠ 10 9 6                        ♠ Q J 8 2
♡ A 10 2            N           ♡ 8 7 6
◇ 9 7          W       E        ◇ 2
♣ J 6 5 4 3        S           ♣ A K 9 7 2
              ♠ 5 3
              ♡ Q 5
              ◇ K 10 8 6 5 4 3
              ♣ Q 10
```

This was the bidding at table 1:

South	West	North	East
Jacoby	Garozzo	Wolff	Belladonna
—	—	—	No
No	No	1♣	No
1♡	No	2♡	No
3♢	No	3♠	No
4♡	No	5♢	No
6♢	No	No	No

The Americans were playing a strong one club and South's one heart response indicated upwards of 7 points. On the surface, it is difficult to see why Jacoby went on over five diamonds. He lost two aces, naturally.

At the other table the Italians were playing Precision. This was their sequence:

South	West	North	East
Bianchi	Blumenthal	Forquet	Goldman
—	—	—	No
No	No	1♣	No
1♢	No	1♡	No
3♢	No	3♠	No
4♡	No	6♡	No
No	No		

The trouble here was that the response of one diamond followed by three diamonds promised a 1-4-4-4 type. Forquet's three spades was ace inquiry, and four hearts promised five controls!

Before the lead, Forquet politely explained the sequence —as he saw it. Goldman led a trump to cut down the ruffs. In with the ace of hearts, Blumenthal had an impossible guess. He returned a spade and Forquet made the slam.

The Beauty of Ocho Rios

The most beautiful single hand in the world championship at
Ocho Rios, Jamaica, occurred in the final, where the women
in the Venice Trophy and the men in the Bermuda Bowl
played the same hands. Only the Swedes and the Chinese,
playing for third place, finished in the right contract on a deal
where the South player held:

♠ A K 7
♡ A K Q 8 4 3
♦ A
♣ A K 8

Whatever system of valuation you use, it was a handsome
collection. You could almost bid a small slam 'in the dark'.

As you would expect, all the South players opened two
clubs, except for Danièle Gaviard, who at the time was
experimenting with a variation proposed by Sam Stayman
whereby the opening on big hands was two diamonds in
preference to two clubs. Don't ask me why.

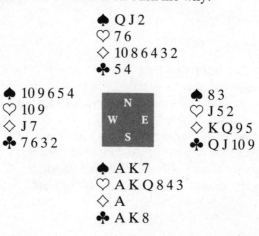

```
              ♠ Q J 2
              ♡ 7 6
              ♦ 10 8 6 4 3 2
              ♣ 5 4
♠ 10 9 6 5 4                    ♠ 8 3
♡ 10 9           N             ♡ J 5 2
♦ J 7        W      E          ♦ K Q 9 5
♣ 7 6 3 2        S             ♣ Q J 10 9
              ♠ A K 7
              ♡ A K Q 8 4 3
              ♦ A
              ♣ A K 8
```

Chevalley and Gaviard stopped in five hearts after this sequence:

Gaviard	Chevalley
2◇	2♡
3♡	3NT
4♣	4♡
4♠	5♡
No	

North, with useful bits, might have shown a little more life after her partner had carried the bidding to the five level on her own. (Still, they did better than the American ladies, Bjerkan and Chambers, who just reached . . . four hearts.)

In the match between Britain and America Flint and Sheehan had, in effect, a similar sequence to the French pair. This time, Jeremy Flint was the one who failed to make any forward move. It looked a certain loss, but at the other table the world champions languished in . . . two clubs!

South	West	North	East
Ross	Forrester	Lawrence	Armstrong
—	—	No	1◇
2♣	No	No	No

East's one diamond opening signified less than 10 points. The American system was that such 'non-existent' opening bids should be ignored; but unfortunately Ross and Lawrence were not a regular pair, Ross's usual partner, Pender, being indisposed. Lawrence, evidently, forgot his instructions.

As often happens in such impossible contracts, the play was funny, too. South won the heart lead and the safest way to eight tricks was to make sure of a diamond ruff in hand. Instead, Ross played three rounds of trumps. Now a low diamond from East, with West unblocking the jack, would have been just fine; but instead East drew a fourth round of trumps, and then South made all the rest of the tricks.

It was an expensive hand for the Americans, but it did not prevent them from winning their sixth Bermuda Bowl.

According to Hoyle

Bridge players everywhere spoke in low voices about the scene that might have occurred after this deal in a game of rubber bridge: a third world war, perhaps.

West was Dr Pierre Jaïs, a young man in 1950. He held:

> ♠ 8 7 5
> ♡ —
> ◇ 8 5 2
> ♣ A K Q J 8 6 4

As dealer, at love all, he decided to pass. No positive bid would have expressed the hand well, and there was a chance that he might spring a surprise later. The bidding continued:

South	West	North	East
—	No	No	No
2♣	5♣	5NT	No
6◇	No	No	No

North, as you will see in a moment, held two aces, and technically his right move was to jump in notrumps, on the analogy of 2♣–3NT, the system response with two aces. However, he decided that a leap to 6NT might prove awkward and chose an ambiguous, but sensible, 5NT. Just as well, for the full hand was:

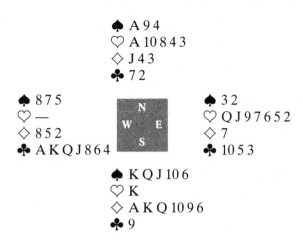

```
              ♠ A 9 4
              ♡ A 10 8 4 3
              ◇ J 4 3
              ♣ 7 2

♠ 8 7 5              ♠ 3 2
♡ —                  ♡ Q J 9 7 6 5 2
◇ 8 5 2              ◇ 7
♣ A K Q J 8 6 4      ♣ 10 5 3

              ♠ K Q J 10 6
              ♡ K
              ◇ A K Q 10 9 6
              ♣ 9
```

What do you suppose that West led against six diamonds? Not difficult, of course, for modern players. He began with the 4 of clubs, the low card inviting a return of the lower of the possible suits, a heart rather than a spade.

Now perhaps you think that East declined to contribute his 10, idly playing low and enabling the declarer to make an overtrick. No, it wasn't that: it was worse!

East won with the 10 of clubs and followed the old Whist principle—*Return your partner's suit.*

There was a hush round the table, while the kibitzers waited for the explosion. The young doctor turned pale, but not a word escaped his lips as he entered the score, then cut the cards for North to deal the next hand. Which perhaps is why his happily unconscious partner has retained his anonymity over the years.

Torn to Shreds

In the European Championship at Salsomaggiore in 1985 the French ladies were brilliantly successful and the Open team was doing well till near the finish. Then in the 17th round France lost to Norway. We had a bye in the next round, for which we were credited 18 points out of 25, and Paul Chemla remarked, 'It's a pity we can't have two more byes—this would be our best chance'. This was prophetic, for France lost both the last two matches. Worst was the 25-5 defeat by the Swiss, who had nothing to lose and were in shooting mood. There was a catastrophe on the following deal:

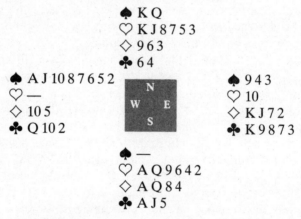

♠ K Q
♡ K J 8 7 5 3
◇ 9 6 3
♣ 6 4

♠ A J 10 8 7 6 5 2
♡ —
◇ 10 5
♣ Q 10 2

♠ 9 4 3
♡ 10
◇ K J 7 2
♣ K 9 8 7 3

♠ —
♡ A Q 9 6 4 2
◇ A Q 8 4
♣ A J 5

East–West were vulnerable and the bidding went:

South	West	North	East
Bernasconi	Soulet	Doche	Lebel
1♡	3♠	4♡	4♠
5◇	No	6♡	No
7♡	No	No	No

North's six hearts looks quite wrong to me; his K Q of spades would be worth very little.

West made the best lead—a club. It looks like two down, doesn't it, since South has a diamond as well as a club loser.

However . . . West chose the 10 of clubs and East did not volunteer his king. One extra trick to the declarer. And then, when South ruffed two spades in hand and ran dummy's trumps, Lebel, still placing the declarer with A Q J x of clubs, discarded two diamonds!

At the other table, where Chemla showed a better appreciation of the North hand, the bidding went:

South	West	North	East
Perron	Collaros	Chemla	Catzeflis
1♥	3♠	4♥	No
4♠	No	5♥	No
6♥	No	No	No

This time West led the 2 of clubs, East had no problem in playing the king, and the declarer had to lose two tricks.

'You defeated the small slam all right on board 25, I suppose?' said Chemla when he rejoined his team-mates.

'Sorry' was the reply. 'We didn't beat the grand slam either.'

PART V

Some Great Problems

These (with one exception) are deals from actual play that present problems almost too difficult to solve at the table. The reader is placed in a no-man's-land where only a great champion might sometimes find the winning line.

Le Pari de Mari*

At one point during a tournament at Marrakesh two French champions, Max Coppolani and Christian Mari, struck a small bet. Convinced that he was right, Mari went to the bar and ordered an anticipatory drink. But perhaps he was a little hasty!

```
                  ♠ A K
                  ♡ A 7 6
                  ◇ 10 4 2
                  ♣ A 10 9 6 2

  ♠ J 9 7 2          N          ♠ Q 10 5 3
  ♡ 8 4         W        E      ♡ Q J 10 3
  ◇ 9 3                         ◇ 8 6 5
  ♣ J 8 7 4 3        S          ♣ K 5

                  ♠ 8 6 4
                  ♡ K 9 5 2
                  ◇ A K Q J 7
                  ♣ Q
```

At love all the bidding went:

South	West	North	East
Coppolani	Jelloui	Moreno	Mari
1◇	No	2♣	No
2◇	No	2♠	No
3NT	No	4◇	No
5◇	No	6◇	all pass

West leads the 3 of diamonds and the question is: Can you make the small slam in diamonds against any defence?

---

* It would be a shame to lose the assonance of the title, which means The Bet of Mari.—T.R.

Mari thought not. You can make eleven tricks by ruffing a spade, obviously, but where will the twelfth come from? By ruffing the second round of clubs, then establishing a trick with the 10 9? No, said Mari, I spoil that little game by ruffing the 10 of clubs.

This seemed to be the end of the matter, but no! There was another line of play—quite simple once you think of it. Even after the trump lead it is possible to make twelve tricks by cross-ruffing.

Win with the jack of diamonds, ruff the second club, cash two spades, ruff another club. Ruff the third spade in dummy, the fourth club in hand. This brings you to:

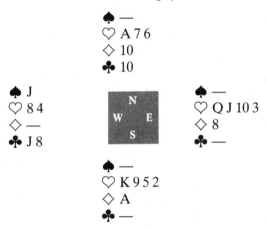

♠ —
♡ A 7 6
♢ 10
♣ 10

♠ J   ♠ —
♡ 8 4   ♡ Q J 10 3
♢ —   ♢ 8
♣ J 8   ♣ —

♠ —
♡ K 9 5 2
♢ A
♣ —

Now you cash king and ace of hearts and no-one can prevent you from making two more tricks with the ace and 10 of trumps.

Point to remember: When you cannot make the tricks you need by straightforward play such as suit establishment, don't overlook the possibility of a complete cross-ruff. This type of play is easy to miss when you have to take several ruffs in the long trump hand.

The Brunswick Coup

One day I had a telephone call from Albert Faigenbaum, a world champion in 1982.

'Hallo, José, I've something that will interest you.'

'I have a pad handy. Go ahead.'

'We were talking about this hand, which had occurred in a match, and Michael Brunswick suggested a solution which the rest of us had missed. It's very pretty and entirely logical.'

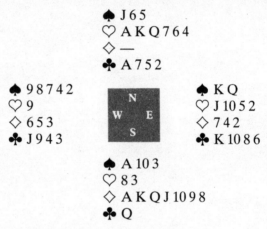

```
              ♠ J 6 5
              ♡ A K Q 7 6 4
              ◇ —
              ♣ A 7 5 2
♠ 9 8 7 4 2                      ♠ K Q
♡ 9                             ♡ J 10 5 2
◇ 6 5 3                          ◇ 7 4 2
♣ J 9 4 3                        ♣ K 10 8 6
              ♠ A 10 3
              ♡ 8 3
              ◇ A K Q J 10 9 8
              ♣ Q
```

The bidding was on these lines:

South	North
—	1♡
2◇	3♣
3♠	4♡
4NT	5♡ (two aces)
7◇	7NT

North transferred to 7NT just in case the diamonds were not solid and the hearts were.

West led the 9 of spades to the queen and ace. How should

South play to make this grand slam?

The spade lead is surprisingly awkward. If West had led a club, for example, there would be twelve tricks on top and the thirteenth would come from a squeeze against East in spades and hearts. South's problem, after the spade lead, is that he cannot cash the ace of clubs and get back to hand to run the diamonds.

Michael Brunswick suggested a brilliant solution, which would work if either defender held four hearts plus the king of spades and the king of clubs. Play six rounds of diamonds, he said, and you reach this ending:

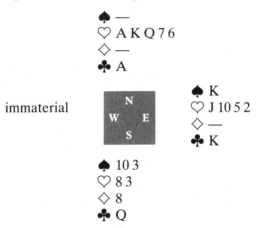

```
              ♠ —
              ♡ A K Q 7 6
              ◇ —
              ♣ A
                            ♠ K
                            ♡ J 10 5 2
immaterial                  ◇ —
                            ♣ K
              ♠ 10 3
              ♡ 8 3
              ◇ 8
              ♣ Q
```

You discard the ace of clubs from dummy on the last diamond and East is caught in a repeating squeeze.

Oddly enough, the discard of the ace of clubs cannot be wrong. If the hearts are not breaking, then the only chance will be to find the player with the long hearts also in control of the two menaces in the black suits.

This deal, or something of the same kind, has been repeated many times in magazine problems, so I am happy to record where the story began.

Point to remember: When you have menace cards in three suits (here the hearts were an extended menace) you may be able to develop two extra tricks from a squeeze.

The Big Fish and the Young Fisherman

The Epson company is a great supporter of bridge, its most famous promotion the world-wide simultaneous pairs. The company also sponsors other big tournaments—among them, a team event in Tokyo. Four young Hungarians asked if they could play and the reply was: 'Certainly. Be our guests at the Hilton.'

The team finished in the middle of the field, but their captain, Szapannos, played a brilliant defence on a deal where North and East held:

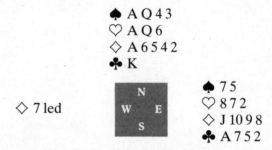

North–South bid to 6NT and Szappanos, East, doubled, not so much because he was confident of beating the contract as because he wanted to discourage his partner from leading one of the major suits. West, as ordered, began with a low diamond through dummy's suit. South cashed the king and queen (West following), then played a club to dummy's king. The question is, how do you plan the defence from this point?

You win with the ace of clubs and . . .

But this is just what you don't do! The ace of clubs won't run away, and if you take this early trick you improve the declarer's chance to bring off a squeeze against your partner. As is well known, a declarer who has, say, eleven tricks on top, will usually improve his chances for a twelfth by conceding one trick as soon as possible.

Now let's see the effect of East's refusal to win with the ace of clubs.

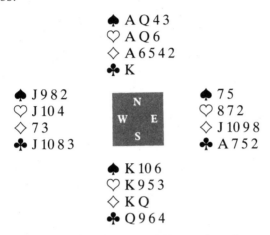

```
                    ♠ A Q 4 3
                    ♡ A Q 6
                    ◇ A 6 5 4 2
                    ♣ K
  ♠ J 9 8 2                         ♠ 7 5
  ♡ J 10 4           N              ♡ 8 7 2
  ◇ 7 3          W       E          ◇ J 10 9 8
  ♣ J 10 8 3         S              ♣ A 7 5 2
                    ♠ K 10 6
                    ♡ K 9 5 3
                    ◇ K Q
                    ♣ Q 9 6 4
```

It is not difficult to see that if East takes the ace of clubs there will be a squeeze for the twelfth trick. West will have to discard twice, once on the ace of diamonds and once on the fourth heart. But after the ace of clubs has been ducked, careful defence will prevail.

Point to remember: Very often the defender will aim to bring about the situation where he can win all the remaining tricks but one. It may be good play for the defenders to prevent this.

Violence at Memphis

The title does not refer to tumultuous events in Arab history, but to the final selection trials held at Memphis, on the banks of the Mississipi. The famous team of Martel-Stansby, Pender-Ross, Hamman-Wolff, led by 100 match points after 45 boards, was 44 behind after 96, and finally won by 5 points, 339 to 334, after 128. American writers called it the most ferocious encounter in the history of bridge.

In the midst of all these fireworks there were many fine coups, the best of all by Bob Hamman, who has won more titles than any other American player.

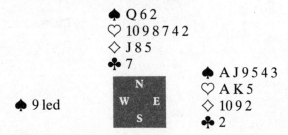

```
                  ♠ Q 6 2
                  ♡ 10 9 8 7 4 2
                  ◇ J 8 5
                  ♣ 7
                                    ♠ A J 9 5 4 3
                           N        ♡ A K 5
                  W        E        ◇ 10 9 2
         ♠ 9 led           S        ♣ 2
```

This was the bidding at game all:

South	West	North	East
Bergen	Wolff	Cohen	Hamman
1♣	No	1♡	2♠
3◇	4♠	No	No
4NT (1)	No	5◇	Dble (2)
No	No	No	

(1) Not conventional, but obviously forward-going.

(2) He is not doubling on the strength of the major-suit honours. His holding in the minors makes it likely that the distribution will be awkward for the declarer, who is marked with a big minor two-suiter.

West led the 8 of spades (third best) and East's jack was ruffed by the declarer. South cashed the ace of clubs, then played a second club, ruffed by dummy's 8 of diamonds. How do you see the defence now? (On the two club leads West has played the 8 and the 10.)

North showed very little in the auction, so South, who has gone to five diamonds almost on his own, must be 5-6 or 5-7 in the minors. On the other hand, it does look as though the clubs are not yet established. Well, to shorten the story, Hamman *did not overruff* the 8 of diamonds. See the effect:

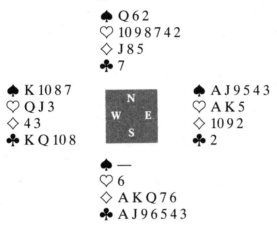

```
                  ♠ Q 6 2
                  ♡ 10 9 8 7 4 2
                  ♢ J 8 5
                  ♣ 7
 ♠ K 10 8 7                      ♠ A J 9 5 4 3
 ♡ Q J 3            N            ♡ A K 5
 ♢ 4 3          W     E          ♢ 10 9 2
 ♣ K Q 10 8         S            ♣ 2
                  ♠ —
                  ♡ 6
                  ♢ A K Q 7 6
                  ♣ A J 9 6 5 4 3
```

Spade lead ruffed, ace of clubs, club ruffed by the 8 of diamonds. Now, if East overruffs and forces the declarer again, South can still ruff a club with the jack of diamonds, draw trumps and concede one club to West; one down.

When the 8 of diamonds was allowed to hold, South exited from dummy with a heart and was forced again in spades. Declarer could ruff the next club with the jack of diamonds, but he had lost control now and was three down, 800. At the other table a trump was led against the same contract and South was two down, 500.

Point to remember: When the declarer is seeking to establish a ponderous two-suiter, a defender with modest length in the trump suit should aim to preserve it.

The Invisible Precaution

Hugh Ross has won the Bermuda Bowl several times, but for some reason one hears less of him than of some of the other world champions. At Monte Carlo in 1976 his team-mates were Eisenberg, Hamilton, Paulsen, I. Rubin and Soloway. In an early match against Australia he landed a slam that was twice defeated at other tables.

♠ A 4
♡ K 9 6 4 2
◇ A J
♣ Q 7 6 3

◇ 6 led

```
      N
  W       E
      S
```

♠ J 7 6 3
♡ A Q
◇ K 5
♣ A K 10 9 8

At love all the bidding went:

South	West	North	East
Ross	Seres	Paulsen	Howard
1♣ (1)	No	1♠ (2)	No
2♣	No	2♡	No
2♠	No	3♣	No
3♡	No	4NT	No
5♡	No	6♣	all pass

(1) Strong club, 17 upwards.
(2) At least 9 points, unbalanced.
West's lead of a low diamond was won by dummy's jack.

When a low club was led from the table East showed out, discarding a spade.

If the trumps had broken 3-1 there would have been no problem: South would draw trumps, discard one spade on the king of hearts, and ruff the third round. With the trumps 4-0 this plan would be awkward, if not impossible. It might be better to give up the spade ruff and aim for four tricks in hearts. The snag was that hearts were 5-1, the full hand being:

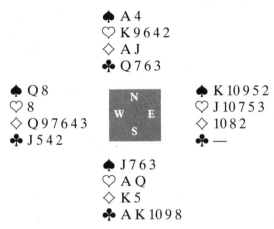

```
              ♠ A 4
              ♡ K 9 6 4 2
              ◇ A J
              ♣ Q 7 6 3
  ♠ Q 8                      ♠ K 10 9 5 2
  ♡ 8              N         ♡ J 10 7 5 3
  ◇ Q 9 7 6 4 3  W   E       ◇ 10 8 2
  ♣ J 5 4 2        S         ♣ —
              ♠ J 7 6 3
              ♡ A Q
              ◇ K 5
              ♣ A K 10 9 8
```

After a diamond lead against six clubs, South plays a club to the ace and finds the 4-0 break.

At the other table, after the same beginning, the Australian declarer played ace and queen of hearts and ran into an immediate ruff. He still had to lose a spade.

There was no hurry to play on the hearts, so Ross drew the trumps in four rounds, then played off ace and queen of hearts. Now a diamond to the ace was more than awkward for East, who was down to three cards in each major. He chose to throw a spade, and then ace and another spade ended the affair. A heart discard by East on the diamond lead would have been no better.

Point to remember: Think always of the worst that can happen and of what you can do if it does happen.

Everything Upside Down

For the first time in this book it has to be admitted that the deal to be discussed is most unlikely ever to have occurred at the table, and still more unlikely to have been played in the manner described. The play was first noted thirty or forty years ago, and I am sure you will agree that it is worth reviving.

See if you can make four spades on the North–South cards, after a club lead from West. East will ruff and return a diamond. Take as long as you like.

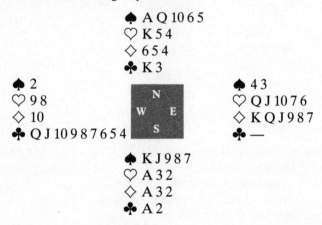

```
                    ♠ A Q 10 6 5
                    ♡ K 5 4
                    ◇ 6 5 4
                    ♣ K 3
  ♠ 2                                    ♠ 4 3
  ♡ 9 8              N                   ♡ Q J 10 7 6
  ◇ 10          W        E               ◇ K Q J 9 8 7
  ♣ Q J 10 9 8 7 6 5 4    S             ♣ —
                    ♠ K J 9 8 7
                    ♡ A 3 2
                    ◇ A 3 2
                    ♣ A 2
```

At love all the bidding might go:

South	West	North	East
1♠	4♣	4♠	No
No	No		

West leads the queen of clubs, you play the king from dummy, and East ruffs. You follow suit with the ace. Naturally.

You win the diamond return, draw the two remaining trumps, and play ace followed by king of hearts. Then you present the lead to West by playing a low, very low, club from each hand.

West, who has only clubs left, must win and play another club. You don't take a ruff-and-discard. Not yet. Instead, you throw a heart from dummy and a diamond from your own hand. This leaves:

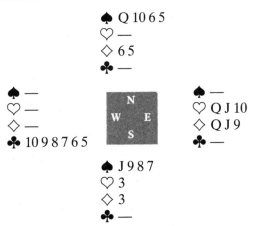

You ruff the next club in dummy and dispose of your remaining diamond. You have made your contract, losing just three tricks. And funnily enough, although you began with K x of clubs opposite A x, the three tricks you have lost have all been in clubs!